More Hidden Women of the Gospels

More Hidden Women of the Gospels

Kathy Coffey

Maryknoll, New York 10545

Founded in 1970, Orbis Books endeavors to publish works that enlighten the mind, nourish the spirit, and challenge the conscience. The publishing arm of the Maryknoll Fathers and Brothers, Orbis seeks to explore the global dimensions of the Christian faith and mission, to invite dialogue with diverse cultures and religious traditions, and to serve the cause of reconciliation and peace. The books published reflect the views of their authors and do not represent the official position of the Maryknoll Society. To learn more about Orbis Books, please visit our website at www.orbisbooks.com.

Published by Orbis Books, Box 302, Maryknoll, NY 10545-0302.

Manufactured in the United States of America
Manuscript editing and typesetting by Joan Weber Laflamme.

Library of Congress Cataloging-in-Publication Data

Names: Coffey, Kathy, author.
Title: More hidden women of the Gospels / Kathy Coffey.
Description: Maryknoll : Orbis Books, 2020. | Includes bibliographical references.
Identifiers: LCCN 2020017087 (print) | LCCN 2020017088 (ebook) | ISBN 9781626983847 (trade paperback) | ISBN 9781608338481 (epub)
Subjects: LCSH: Women in the Bible. | Bible. Gospels.—Biography. | Bible. Acts.—Biography.
Classification: LCC BS2445 .C5936 2020 (print) | LCC BS2445 (ebook) | DDC 226/.0922082—dc23
LC record available at https://lccn.loc.gov/2020017087
LC ebook record available at https://lccn.loc.gov/2020017088

For my granddaughters:

Louisa Jackson
Maya Ileane
Amahlia Kathleen
Claire Victoreen

This small offering in love.

Contents

Part III
Women in Acts

Part IV
Group Resources

Introduction

No other era in history has been researched and described as thoroughly as the time of Jesus. Archeologists, scripture scholars, historians, musicians, and artists have all explored the context of that era. This is an exploration of another kind, one of the imagination. It seeks to uncover more women who moved through Jesus's world as they do through ours, but whose stories sadly have been overlooked.

The women of the New Testament were a secret treasure that I first imagined in *Hidden Women of the Gospels.* The present book is a sequel that follows a similar pattern. To recreate these biblical women's stories, I have used a Midrash technique to enhance the biblical stories, imaginatively filling in blank spaces, expanding on underdeveloped or missing events, or casting them in a contemporary setting or language. Midrash explores the Bible not through analysis but through imagination.

In other words, there's more to wonder about than our limited, time- and space-bound human perspective can reveal. "In more theological or religious terms it is the Midrash, the underlying truth, the inspired layers that are hinted at, that invite but do not force themselves upon us. They must be searched out, struggled with and taken to heart. It is, at root, the mystery that makes the story memorable, worth telling over and over again, and staking your life on it."[1]

[1] Megan McKenna and Tony Cowan, *Keepers of the Story* (Maryknoll, NY: Orbis Books, 1997), 66.

The first book's popularity came from readers who were delighted to discover unknown, imagined stories about people remarkably like themselves despite the centuries that stretched between them. To my great delight, that book appealed across denominational and gender lines. It led to my giving retreats and talks in Catholic, Episcopal, Methodist, Lutheran, and Presbyterian church communities, both nationally and internationally.

Some religious institutions tend to enshrine "the way we've always done it" and may be slightly rattled to think of beloved Bible figures as feminine. But we know, for instance, that there were women shepherds at the time of Jesus, as there still are in many parts of the world. What a great service, expanding the images of male and female children, their parents and parishes, Fontanini (an Italian company, imported to the United States by Roman, Inc.) did when it included women figures in its crèche sets, large ones for churches, small ones for homes.

Many people remember only one woman in their childhood crèche; Mary was the token female, and the gender of the angels was unclear. So, too, much art portrays the beloved figure of the Good Shepherd as male (Jn 10:1–18). Yet it's not impossible to imagine a woman shepherd seeking the lost sheep. How many women have gone out of their way for the balky patient, the irritating student, the offspring, or a nephew or niece or grandchild who's wandered into addiction or crime? As a new awareness of women sweeps the world, this inclusion of women in the Bible has much to contribute.

In my first hunt for women who were erased or forgotten in the scriptural accounts, I missed a few. The stories that once eluded me now clamor to be told. It reminds me of a day when my six grandchildren were playing hide-and-seek. Those under four didn't quite get the concept; from within a closet a small voice pleaded, "Find me! Find me!" That might work in other ways: first, the hidden women awaiting discovery; and second, God wanting us to seek God through a different lens or an imagined woman's life experience.

So the title applies not only to the quantity of women but to those more deeply hidden. The first book detailed the "low-hanging fruit," and this one the deeper treasures, but together they work in concert to achieve the same goal: to offer the world of the New Testament through a feminine lens. How did women experience and view familiar events? These stories are always told in first-person point of view, for immediacy. All the women in the previous book were given names. In this book not all are named, so perhaps we could all identify with "the woman who called out" or "the woman who caught crumbs." For women who lack an entry to the Bible where all the characters in the story are male, this approach opens doors.

Historical Jesus and Universal Christ

It's important to differentiate the historical person, Jesus of Nazareth, from the cosmic Christ. On the one hand, Jesus is a carpenter and teacher who lived in chronological time with the usual human constraints: fatigue, hunger, thirst, and frustration. He was born in Bethlehem of Judea and crucified outside Jerusalem. The women we can imagine meeting Jesus found him initially quite ordinary—no neon lights or extraordinary powers set him apart.

On the other hand, the cosmic Christ is not limited by time and space but is omnipresent, revealing God everywhere. Jesus arose still Jesus but also with divinity that he shares with all humanity. He could be in two places at once, pass through walls and locked doors, still with a physical presence but in a different form. He is personal but sometimes hard to recognize.

Like the "perfect unity of the human Jesus with the divine Christ"[2] so humans "share the divine nature" (2 Pet 1:4). The "divine DNA" is held in all creatures, so all creation praises God.

---

[2] Richard Rohr, *The Universal Christ: How a Forgotten Reality Can Change Everything We See, Hope for, and Believe* (New York: Convergent Books, 2019), 29.

Jesus says he is the light of the world (Jn 8:12), but he also tells people, "You are the light of the world" (Mt 5:14). Jesus calls forth the divine in the women he encounters; they are free to welcome or reject that call, or simply remain puzzled, still works in progress. In one way or another they meet his forgiveness, his invitation to fullness without respect to gender.

He brings them more alive and teaches them to trust and reflect on their own unique experience. Because he values his own human experience and bases his teaching on it, he brings them to appreciate *their* leaven, *their* lamps, lost coins, bread and wine, children, flowers and vineyards. Women who learned from Jesus would agree: "From his fullness we have all received, grace upon grace" (Jn 1:16).

ENLARGED STORIES

This book has three primary areas of focus. The first is the stories of people who actually appear in the Gospels. If their gender was unclear in those texts, I've opted to make them feminine. After centuries of framing them as masculine, it seems time to reverse the trend. Bright, feisty, lively women surrounded Jesus—and certainly didn't ask permission to touch his hem or anoint his head. It's also time to speculate about the "supporting actresses." Who knows whether Zacchaeus had a daughter or Bartimaeus a wife? When there's no definite answer, imagine away!

FEMININE METAPHOR AND PARABLE

One area I hadn't explored in the previous book was Jesus's use of feminine metaphor. Because he was so beautifully balanced, integrating the best of male and female, he could draw on the world of women for dramatic comparisons. When a subject—like the kingdom of heaven—is unfamiliar to an audience, the finest speakers compare it to something familiar, for instance, the gradual growth of leaven in dough. In Jesus's era men didn't cook. But women would have nodded in agreement, perhaps astonished that someone understood their world.

Another unexplored territory was the women in the parables. While these are stories, they ring so true they must have had some foundation in reality. Jesus was the most creative person who ever lived. But like any other human, his imagination had to be grounded in the life around him and the people he knew. He didn't draw his stories from Neptune or Jupiter but from human experience, half of which is feminine. He must have overheard a frantic woman thwacking her broom vigorously in search of a coin, or a young girl sobbing because she'd been locked out of the wedding feast. He lived close to humanity in a world of patches on garments, religious hypocrites, stupid bureaucrats, recalcitrant relatives, empty wine jars at wedding feasts, risky gambles. He heard the anguished scream as often as the chanted psalm. He knew how human life can be kind as well as terrible.

Jesus was a keen observer of the daily life around him, the flow of humanity in relationship: master and servant, man and woman, parent and child. No human experience was foreign to him. With his keen sensitivity he would never ignore or exclude half the human race. Instead, he shaped his dominant metaphors from women's experience: leaven in dough, patches on cloth, lamps on stands, vines and branches, washing feet, and drawing water. All came from the feminine world, women's "image bank." He lifted their relationships, challenges, joys, and daily drudgery into a glimpse of God's reign.

While some might criticize this "enrichment" of the parables, it's important to understand that Jesus stood firmly within the *mashal* tradition—the Jewish branch of a universal tradition that valued the sacred story, poem, riddle, or dialogue as the path to wisdom. (We can think of other examples among other world religions: the Sufis, Greeks, Buddhists, Hindus, and so on.) This stream of teaching was more interested in inner transformation than in priesthood, prophecy, or politics.[3] It came closer to what Anthony de Mello said: "You have yet to understand, my dears, that the shortest distance between a human being and Truth is a story."[4] Because Jesus knew the profound effect of story, it's hard to imagine that this embellishment of his originals for a later audience would bring him anything but delight.

THE BOOK OF ACTS

Who else but the women would gather the people, tell the story, and bake the bread? The early community of faith was filled with feminine influence: unnamed women at Pentecost, Lydia, Dorcas, Priscilla, the earliest leaders and organizers. They may be slightly known, but the missing element, which can be imagined, is their inner life. "What fascinating chapters must be missing from our history," says Florence Gillman.[5] But we needn't mourn an absence when we can create a presence. It's a different technique from that some scholars use, but ancient Midrash was a creative transmission, adapting ancient sources to contemporary time and place. Scripture is a rich source of meaning that can be discovered through probing and broadening the text.

Due to the "radical lack of knowledge about females in early Christianity . . . women's stories cannot escape a tentativeness which comes from having to employ much speculation, even imagination."[6] The imagination has held an honored place throughout Christian history, especially uplifted by Saint Joan of Arc and Saint Ignatius. Midrash was used by Jewish rabbis long before Christians adapted it.

---

[3] Cynthia Bourgeault, *The Wisdom Jesus: Transforming Heart and Mind—A New Perspective on Christ and His Message* (Boulder, CO: Shambhala, 2008), 23–24.

[4] Anthony de Mello, *One Minute Wisdom* (New York: Doubleday, 1986), 23.

[5] Florence Gillman, *Women Who Knew Paul* (Collegeville, MN: Liturgical Press, 1992), 70.

[6] Gillman, *Women Who Knew Paul*, 14–15.

> The rabbis, like modern readers, often found the text of the Bible obscure, and in general recognized that scripture spoke with an economy of language. . . . The biblical narratives had to be updated, ethical and cultural perspectives modernized, and new tales composed out of the silence of scripture. By means of midrash, the Bible was wrapped in the garment of contemporary perceptions, issues and concerns, and thus transformed; in turn the contemporary world was perceived in the light of scripture, and thereby illuminated.[7]

WHY BOTHER?

Those who practice yoga, or anyone trying to achieve balance, discover how hard it is to stand on one foot. If prompted to do so for a prolonged stretch, we inevitably wobble, reach for the wall, or crash unceremoniously. There may be an analogy here to a church that for centuries has tried to stand on one male foot. Imagining the women's stories, including them in homilies, sermons, newsletters, retreats, workshops, and bulletins, might restore a much needed balance.

As we make these efforts and explore the scriptures, bear in mind that we move in mystery, remembering what Albert Einstein said, "The most beautiful thing we can experience is the mysterious. . . . It is the source of all true art and all science. He to whom the emotion is a stranger, who can no longer pause to wonder, and stand rapt in awe, is as good as dead—his eyes are closed."[8]

This effort to imagine the women in the Gospels follows Jesus's model. He never took the oppressive, "putting down" role of other men in his era, disparaging women. His treatment of women, befriending, including and learning from them, departed from cus-

---

[7] *Interpreter's Dictionary of the Bible* (Nashville, TN: Abingdon, 1985), 595.

[8] Albert Einstein, *Living Philosophies* (New York: Simon and Schuster, 1931).

tom in a culture where the rabbis taught that it would be "better that the Torah be burned than placed in the mouth of a woman." How dramatically he broke the taboos; how farsightedly he called people to a larger vision of God's reign. Only an extraordinary man, one who lived the full spectrum of humanity, could compare his approaching passion to a woman's pain in labor, her joy in a child's birth (Jn 16:21). How it must have saddened him to hear the traditional proverb: "When a boy child comes, peace comes. When a girl child comes, nothing comes." How could his contemporaries so utterly discount half of God's creation? To what extent do we, centuries later, continue that affront? "Enough!" said Jesus, and began a revolution in attitudes toward and recognition of women that has still not been fully achieved.

QUESTIONS FOR REFLECTION AND DISCUSSION

This book isn't restricted to stories or metaphors, but it provides launching pads for personal reflection and discussion. Perhaps a story will prompt a new way of thinking about the scripture or one's own experience. The questions that follow each story help us to take ownership of the material. In reading scripture we see a wide spectrum of responses to Jesus. As in the words of John's Prologue:

> He was in the world, and the world came into being through him; yet the world did not know him. He came to what was his own, and his own people did not accept him. But to all who received him, who believed in his name, he gave power to become children of God, who were born, not of blood or of the will of the flesh or of the will of man, but of God. And the Word became flesh and lived among us, and we have seen his glory, the glory as of a father's only son, full of grace and truth. (Jn 1:10–14)

Some accept him and respond immediately, like Mary at the annunciation; others question him, like Martha after Lazarus's death, or understand more gradually, as did the woman at the well or Nicodemus. Still others never have a glimmer, and even Jesus grows exasperated, asking Philip: "Have I been with you all this time, Philip, and you still do not know me?"

In this book each woman meets and receives Jesus according to her own circumstances, personality, gifts, background, and so forth. As in canonical texts, some come quickly; others wonder or waver; others never seem to understand. Transpose Jesus's effect into the world of art. Picture the miners painted by van Gogh, the ballerinas portrayed by Degas, or Toulouse-Lautrec's dancers, singers, prostitutes, and laundresses, vivid spots of flashing color against the dark suits and top hats of the men who surround them. We may speculate on their stories but never really know them as well as we know ourselves. And ultimately, the question is not only do *they* get Jesus's message, but do *I*? The questions provided at the end of each chapter are for individuals to take ownership of the material, either through personal reflection or group discussion. Jesus's primary focus was personal transformation. In his probing conversation with the Samaritan woman or his witty exchange with the Canaanite woman, he wasn't preaching doctrine. As Cynthia Bourgeault notes, "The hallmark of these wisdom teachers was their use of pithy sayings, puzzles, and parables rather than prophetic pronouncements or divine decree. They spoke to people in the language that people spoke, the language of story rather than law."[9]

We may think of Jesus as a priest, but he didn't do well with the religious structures of his day. He was kicked out of a synagogue and almost thrown over a cliff, people were so angry with him.[10] The religious authorities harassed him as he taught and ultimately turned him over to Pilate as a criminal deserving death. Nor was he a prophet, particularly interested in overthrowing the Roman occupation.

---

[9] Bourgeault, *The Wisdom Jesus*, 23–24.

[10] See Chapter 9 of this book, "Stowaway in the Synagogue."

But his vital interest in each person's dignity, becoming the most she could be, is revealed in a procession of characters who enflesh 1 John 3:1: "See what love the Father has given us, that we should be called children of God; and that is what we are." "That is what we are" is what Frederick Buechner calls "the curt monosyllables of fact."[11] These five short words contain the essence of Jesus's message. And all the stories come down to these many faces of Jesus in and through women, the mighty daughters of God.

GROUP RESOURCES

Some people may want to use *More Hidden Women of the Gospels* in a group: a book club, a community retreat, a class, any gathering where the resources in the last section may be helpful. These monologues (with one exception) are shorter versions of some chapters that appear in Parts I, II, and III, because a whole chapter might be too long to read aloud or follow by ear. The shorter versions give the gist of the character and serve as discussion starters. Specific directives appear with some. All entail finding one or more people who are skillful at reading aloud and giving them time to read through the monologue in advance—which should take only a few minutes.

The monologues can certainly be adapted to a particular setting, and some of the guidelines for use include having group members interview the character with their own questions; having the character chat with someone who was important in her life, played by another group member; asking about her relationship to Jesus, including when they first met, and how the relationship developed—or failed to develop. Dramatizing scripture or playing with different angles on it isn't irreverent; indeed, it can make it more relevant to our day and age, our current concerns.

---

[11] Frederick Buechner, *The Faces of Jesus* (New York: Riverwood/ Simon and Schuster, 1974), 128.

Laughter is always welcome as we try to adapt, having fun in bringing ourselves to the ancient texts—and them to us.

The Book of Nehemiah records an interesting response to scripture. When Ezra the priest reads it aloud to the people "from daybreak until midday," one might expect them to doze off or get hungry. Instead, they weep aloud, because they haven't quite measured up to it. Not the response the leaders intended. They've survived the Babylonian captivity, so Nehemiah and Ezra encourage them: "Go your way, eat the fat and drink sweet wine and send portions of them to those for whom nothing is prepared . . . and do not be grieved, for the joy of the LORD is your strength" (Neh 8:10). The people throw a party and "make great rejoicing" because they've understood the Bible anew. Perhaps women should feast too, discovering how validated and important they are in texts that may have seemed distant or exclusionary. Knowing Jesus's welcome to women, let's rejoice. Celebrate!

PART I

WOMEN IN THE GOSPELS

1

Pass the Baby—Anna the Prophetess

(Luke 2:36–38)

My favorite prayer had been one of the psalms, and I lived long enough to see it answered:

> One thing I asked of the Lord,
> that will I seek after:
> to live in the house of the Lord
> all the days of my life,
> to behold the beauty of the Lord,
> and to inquire in God's temple. (Ps 27:4)

Among my friends, I alone seemed uniquely drawn to the temple, the beauty of its spaces and the order of its rituals. The music, the fall of light through high arches, the language of promise: I relished it all. Away from the commotion of the city and the dust of the road, I could recall in peace the happiest years of my life: the seven of my marriage, especially the birth of our child. Before Lilia's birth four barren years had convinced us we couldn't have children. Her coming was such a gift that I'd spend the rest of my life washed with gratitude.

The baby in the temple that day had the same coloring as Lilia; I reached instinctively to hold that small bundle. His weight in my arms, his wispy hair brought back the memories like a flood. The parents seemed awkward country people, unaccustomed to the huge temple, intimidated by the laws, priests, and unfamiliar customs. But the mother knew how to say a gracious "yes," and she handed over her little one trustingly. Or maybe she was in shock. She'd be pierced by a *sword*? What kind of affirmation is *that* for an unsure new mother? So I wanted to compensate and console, directing the conversation back to where it belonged: to thanking God.

In later years, they'd call me a mystic. I just knew that my thanks often welled up and spilled into praise. Allow me to brag in retrospect: I was great-grandmother to Hildegard, Mechtild, Julian of Norwich, so many others whose names are forgotten. Julian lived over seventy years, and during her lifetime experienced "the Black Death, the Hundred Years' War, papal schism, assassinations of a king and an archbishop . . . and so on, [but] she makes not a single mention of any of those events." Instead, she became "irrelevant," listening to the "extraordinarily peaceful, powerful meaning of the love of the one who wants to speak to us, who is entirely without wrath, and because of the serenity of whose power we need be afraid of nothing at all."[1] Luke wrote that I "never left the temple." Maybe I carried it within. After today, I marvel that one frail person can carry so much light.

Anna Today

In healthy families with several small children, a delicate dance ensures that each gets the attention he or she craves. Usually, the loudest gets the most, so mom cuddles the whining three-year-old while dad takes care of the baby. Or, to increase complexity, dad builds Legos with the four-year-old, mom draws with the

[1] James Alison, *Undergoing God* (New York: Continuum, 2006), 31–32.

two-year-old, and grandma/grandpa/older sibling gets the infant. The youngest child is at the bottom of the pecking order and is often the most compliant. As long as the belly is full, the infant can be placed into any available arms, just so they are welcoming and not too bony. Most babies ask little and are delighted by the slightest coo or funny face. No banquets for them—milk will do.

What's astonishing is how *Jesus* takes this place, inverting hierarchy, as Mary, Joseph, Simeon, and Anna play "pass the baby." The Creator of the vast universe, mountains, seas, and stars isn't consulted as he's handed off to strangers who say even stranger things about him.

On December 28, 2014, Pope Francis linked Anna and Simeon to grandparents. Beyond all the sweet fluff of grandparenting, for some there is also the atonement factor. Perhaps the second time around is a chance to make up for haphazard parenting. Young people are *busy*!—jobs to do; meals to cook; careers to pursue; laundry to wash; houses to clean; deadlines to meet; and bills to pay. And in all that frenzy, it's easy to miss how infinitely precious children are. However, grandparents know. Call them dotty, but they've been sidelined to the really important work: cradling, soothing, rocking, and humming. It's a "hidden way" of life; its immense fulfillment not publicized. As Martin Luther King Jr. is often attributed with saying, "If I cannot do great things, I can do small things in a great way."

So when grandparents share their stories, the wealth pours forth. One speaks of a difficult divorce when their grandsons were eight and ten. Distraught themselves, the grandparents were unsure how to help the boys through a major upheaval. Wisely, they followed a friend's advice: "You're not their therapists; you're their grandparents. So do what you've always done." And that role proved a steadying, grounding force for the boys. With major upheavals in their lives, they could count on one sure source of love and affirmation.

Another grandson, who was caring for his neighbor's chickens, called his grandparents in desperation when he arrived one day to find nothing but blood and feathers. His parents were at work, so who *else* would he ask to bring the plastic bags, scoop up the mess, reassure him, and dispose of the remains?

Long-distance grandparents on video calls; grandparents caught in custody battles; grandparents heartbroken because they're barred from seeing their grandchildren; grandparents with more time and money to enjoy children than when they themselves were parents: the stories abound. But what gives them depth and resonance is their echo back to that temple in Jerusalem where two old people waited for they knew not what.

As James Alison points out, when God enters the temple, it's almost off stage, only the minority report of Luke.[2] Not the razzle-dazzle of the main altar or the chief priest, but a side aisle. No opulent vestments, but the warmth Jesus had known before: the cradle of a woman's arms. Thea Bowman adds, Mary and Joseph "didn't need the recognition of the high priest or the approval of the chief magistrate to know that Jesus was a gift from God."[3]

A three-year-old entering a vast baroque cathedral for the first time at Christmas, seeing the trees, banners, huge statues, a jillion tiny white lights, and glittering mosaics arching overhead into infinite space, tightly grasped his mother's hand on one side and his grandmother's on the other. In all that magnificent, awesome space, which tends to dwarf someone three-feet tall, he clung to the human anchors, the warm touch, the reassurance of familiar scents and skin. So too, the temple must have been intimidating to a family from Galilee; even before it was finished, the disciples marveled at its jewels and arches, and couldn't believe Jesus's prediction of its imminent destruction.

How beautifully Luke transposes the whole drama from vastness into human scale. The only tableau that matters is composed of two couples, one old, one younger, centered on an infant.

---

[2] Alison, 102–3.

[3] Celestine Cepress, ed., *Sister Thea Bowman, Shooting Star: Selected Writings and Speeches* (Winona, MN: St. Mary's Press, 1993), 90–91.

The research of women scripture scholars adds to the contemporary appreciation of Anna. Barbara Reid explains that her seven years with her husband evokes the ideal wife, as seven was the number for perfection or completion in biblical symbolism. The same phrase is used for her that would later be used also for Jesus: she fasts and prays. The Greek term for widow (*chera*) means "left empty." But one suspects that her days are far from empty. As this portrait indicates, she fills them with the marvelous presence of the divine. So when her time comes, and a small family enters her turf, she's ready.

Reid believes that Anna, Mary, and Elizabeth continue the line of the powerful prophets of Israel. After Anna, women speak in pain or are corrected or disbelieved. (The shift could be due to separate gospel sources.) Later women became quiet and private—adapting to women's low status in the Greco-Roman world.[4]

Pheme Perkins notes that before Anna only four women in scripture—Miriam (Ex 15:20), Deborah (Judg 4:4–10), Hulda (2 Kings 22:1–20), and Isaiah's wife (Isa 8:3)—have been honored with the name prophetess. Anna has an esteemed ancestry, has spent a lifetime preparing for this moment, has waited almost intolerably long for her chance, and now one naturally expects her to break into a canticle like Simeon's. Yet there is no direct quote, perhaps because "we already know the music she sings."[5]

Anna is the patron saint of those whose language speaks through care, the grandparents who sing off-key lullabies, hunched over a precious lump in crib or arms, the backstage crew, the meticulous researchers who painstakingly prepare the way for the breakthrough discovery but receive no credit themselves. She also could model for those who wait—sometimes interminably long—but don't lose hope.

---

[4] Barbara Reid, *Women in the Gospel of Luke* (Collegeville, MN: Liturgical Press, 1996), 94–95.

[5] Pheme Perkins, "Anna: Waiting a Lifetime," *Give Us This Day* 12 (2013): 318–19.

As Mary Stommes has noted, Anna knew her eighty-four years was just a blip on the timeline of salvation history. However, "it is best not to underestimate the potential of a prophetic blip, especially that of an octogenarian who spends her every waking—and apparently, sleeping—moment in prayer."[6]

Anna's position in Luke's Gospel is exquisitely artful. In her undramatic way Anna becomes the threshold to the next quiet chapter of Jesus's life, about which we know little except that he "grew and became strong, filled with wisdom; and the favor of God was upon him" (Lk 2:40). In the years that followed that day in the temple, did Anna think of him, growing in an obscure town, apparently with no stage larger than a little village, no publicity, and no obvious mission?

Anna, of all people, knew the gift of gradual gestation, almost unnoticed, that would flower in her moment and his ministry. Just as the woman who anointed Jesus launched him toward his passion, giving him beauty for the ordeal ahead, so too Anna signaled the spectacular power that coiled beneath the apparently unimpressive surface. Had she spoken in twenty-first-century jargon, she might have winked conspiratorially and said, "Stay tuned!"

QUESTIONS FOR REFLECTION AND DISCUSSION

1. *Youth knows the rules; old age, the exceptions.* How has an older person helped you come to insight or how have you achieved more wisdom as you've aged?

2. Simeon rightly predicts the disasters ahead for the infant Jesus, but Anna shifts the tone back to praise. Have you seen women do similar things in conversation? How do they do it? Can you give an example?

3. We, too, may wait, seemingly forever. As Mary Stommes says, "We wait for an end to all the violence done to children to-

[6] Mary Stommes, "Wrapped in Joy and Sorrow," *Give Us This Day* 2 (February 5, 2019): 5.

day, in whom the Child Jesus lives on. *Still* he suffers: Child trafficking, sexual abuse by clergy and others, gun violence, which often kills the most vulnerable, the horrific treatment around the world of child refugees." For what do you wait? What gives you hope if the waiting seems to drag on too long?

4. Anna could be the patron saint of widows, grandparents, visionaries. Compose a prayer to her. Here's a start; add your own thoughts:

Anna, help us to "come forward" when it is our *moment, recognizing when the time is ripe, not squandering our power with too much chatter. Help us to embrace and praise the Christ hidden to everyone else, but clear to us. Be a special guide to those who have lost a spouse, filling the emptiness of their loss with the birth of new and totally unexpected life. Comfort those who have waited too long for relief, whose hearts begin to grow stony.*

2

A Servant at Cana—Chloe

(JOHN 2:1–11)

My toes curled, I tell you.
Watching burgundy sheen
lapping the limpid water,
tinting the stone. A blush
warmed my own limbs.

There'd been commotion,
a woman's voice so earnest
I hurried: not the usual crisis.
The steward clueless as always.
Before he even tasted, I knew:

this was good stuff. Now I
extend my empty glass,
yearning for your wine.
Color my diluted days again.
If water glows like ruby, so can I.

In my world, being a woman *and* a servant was the double whammy. Long, exhausting days faded numbly into one another;

each identical to the last. No wonder we anticipated a wedding, even though it meant more work. At a wedding banquet, people who never feasted get to eat more than they'd ever dreamed. Even we servants sneaked more food. From a meager diet we plunged into seven days of eating. For once, we all felt *full.*

Filling the six heavy stone jars with water was backbreaking. My aching arms were stiff, but the woman's voice that I overheard in the crowd was unique. She didn't speak loudly, but the force of her conviction was powerful. Usually, I'd question her order—as she was just an ordinary guest—but something mysterious compelled me to follow her command: "Do whatever he tells you." What had she said to her son, or he to her?

What force of his hand shifted the color in the water jar? Was he an artist? A magician? I had no idea, but still, crazy-hopeful, I sneaked a ladleful. That unexpected wine surpassed anything I had ever tasted!

Sipping it, I understood for the first time what the rabbis had always taught. Marriage was a symbol of the relationship between Israel and God. I'd always loved the promise God made through Isaiah of rich food and well-aged wines (Isa 25:6). I could picture it because I'd served at a few of those feasts. But I never thought *I* was invited to the banquet.

Now, with incomparable deliciousness filling my mouth, I thought *God chose me.* From the beginning of time God sought me like a bride. Always God's compassionate hand had reached out to me. Maybe it was through a friend or an angle of light as I walked home after a long day. Maybe it was morning energy after exhaustion or my reliable good health. My name means "green herb," and I felt the vital juice running through me. Words couldn't capture my awe, but water turned into wine could. This odd intoxication wasn't the usual drunk. It lasted for a long time.

Life afterward became dull again. The daily grind repeated endlessly, grueling hand-to-mouth survival with no relief in sight. But I would remember how the colorless water became effervescent. I carried that taste within.

The steward said something in that rare moment when he was alert: "You had saved the best wine until now." At first, I just wanted to keep drinking. And then I wanted that quiet guest to do it again and again, like magic. But gradually I discovered a new way of seeing, or tasting. Maybe the change hadn't been to the water, but to my taste buds. Now I could see the beauty in ordinary things, taste the deliciousness even in cold water or a fresh orange.

Just when I thought I might be getting used to this radical about-face attitude, a friend told me a story from that surprising wedding guest, whose name I learned later was Jesus. He shocked people when he told the story of the servants being served (Lk 12:35–40). This Jesus seemed to have an odd affinity with us bottom-of-the-heap sorts. A master acting as a servant? The rumors even said he called *himself* a servant. Almost as if God cared about folding sheets and blankets or mopping the mess on the floor! Maybe it's not so startling. Jesus also said only the "little ones" get it (Mt 11:25). Couldn't get much littler than me!

Most of my life, I'd heard "No!" or "Of course not; you're a girl" or "No way; you're a servant!" or "Who do you think you are, the empress?"

Now, after that dramatic shift of water into wine, I don't feel so belittled and denied. I can picture an endless series of rooms opening up, each doorway marked yes. I walk nobly through the arches, sipping a glass of "that wine." Strong and confident, I wonder what powerful effect this stranger has had on me.

Once I stood high above the Sea of Galilee. The view down into that blue bowl, rimmed with violet hills, contained all the beauty of the world. Now I see why it resonated so deeply. That vast lake, like the liquid that filled the ladle, was an image of who God is, deeper than any depth—and who I am, radiant mirror of the divine. When the rabbis or my boss tell me I'm evil and filled to the brim with putrid sin, I close my eyes for a minute and return to the taste of loveliness that better shows who I most truly am.

Now I wonder if the wine was in his words. It's as if he said, "I don't want you to ever feel small."

THE MASTER WHEN HE COMES . . . (LK 12:35–40)

Not probing the silver with
white-gloved finger nor
inspecting sad hearts
saluting at attention.
Not pulling dressing
from raw wounds nor
exposing wrongs better buried.

Flushed from a wedding,
he serves a meal.
The startled servant
keeps trying to rise,
then sinks into comfort
of the warm, full plate,
the master refilling wine.

CANA TODAY

The Cana story shows Jesus's ministry beginning in a small, personal, family setting, not in an institution. He's not in a starring role but is simply an invited guest. The first witnesses to the first miracle are servants, not rabbis or people in authority. God is at work especially in the "intimate daily places of human lives."[1]

The narrative also reveals how the gifts of male and female can come together fruitfully—not only in marriage, but also in the Mary/Jesus, parent/child relationship. Imagine a chorus beautifully blending altos and sopranos.

It all begins when Mary breaks a huge taboo in a society rigidly split along gender lines. To speak with Jesus, she must cross from

[1] Carol Newsome and Sharon Ringe, eds. *The Women's Bible Commentary* (Louisville, KY: Westminster/John Knox Press, 1992), 295.

the "girls' side" of the room to the "boys' side," a divide that still exists at some Orthodox Jewish and Muslim celebrations today (or in the cringing memory of the junior-high dance!). Without a word, Mary dismisses artificial divisions in several swift steps.

Mary also models the ideal parent of a young adult. She doesn't deluge her son with an avalanche of words, as some of us are ever-so-slightly inclined to do. Instead, she simply states the need: they have no wine.

Beneath Jesus's apparent refusal—"My hour has not yet come"—Mary senses his cooperation. She must trust him immensely because, before he's ever agreed to act, she notifies the servants to "do whatever he tells you." As before at the annunciation, God waits on human participation to enact divine and mighty deeds. It first requires *her* noticing and then *her* request, unsurprisingly in the hospitality department where women often excel. Mary also models the stance of prayer. Many words are unnecessary; God understands the need.

And *then* can come an avalanche of grace. Into every relationship, not only marriage, flow droplets of surprising change. Bland water glimmers with hints of wine. We may think this friendship or this community or these siblings have grown stale and tired. Then some miraculous laughter dances across weary eyes or enters familiar voices, and we remember why we've always loved them. Or a crisis occurs that helps us see them in a more appreciative light. To lose one of them would be to lose a part of ourselves.

The Cana miracle can still occur in settings where youthful vigor isn't necessarily present. Touching stories of Alzheimer's patients abound, but this one seems like a sequel titled "Cana: Fifty Years Later." It all began when a man told his parish priest that the following week would mark his fiftieth anniversary. He didn't plan to celebrate, because his wife's Alzheimer's was far advanced. Though he visited her daily, she didn't recognize him.

"But of course you must celebrate!" protested the priest. And within a week, a party came together. She got a permanent wave and a pale blue chiffon dress, which draped gracefully over her wheelchair. He got a haircut and wore his best suit. Twenty-five friends, children, and grandchildren assembled around a large cake.

And in front of them all, he dropped to one knee and repeated his wedding vows. She was more interested in the cake, but that didn't make it less meaningful. In some mysterious way his fidelity was a sign that "you have kept the good wine until now." Perhaps when the appearances of youth, beauty, or brilliance have faded, the gold nugget of enduring love shines most true. As Marcus Borg writes, "The story of Jesus is about a wedding banquet at which the wine never runs out."[2] And the best comes last.

QUESTIONS FOR REFLECTION AND DISCUSSION

1. This chapter contains poetry. Some experiences are so vast that they can't be contained in ordinary vessels. Joy bursts beyond the bounds of prose, falling better into poetic lines or music. Imagine being the servant girl who watched the wine gradually color. How does it change her whole identity and perspective? A later insight might help explain what happened to her: "So you are no longer a slave but a child, and if a child then also an heir, through God" (Gal 4:7).

2. Perhaps some complex dilemma you face now awaits resolution—maybe needing you to invite God, through prayer, to enter it. Try phrasing the situation in about five words, as Mary did for Jesus.

3. For the people of Jesus's day, abundance was often expressed through metaphors of feasts and food, because they probably felt hunger often. What might make a better metaphor for our day, when many still go hungry while many others are overfed?

4. Where have you experienced scarcity turning to abundance, even if it was mostly in your outlook?

5. Have you heard much bombast from religious authorities, as this servant girl did, hammering away at faults?, Or has

---

[2] Marcus Borg, *Reading The Gospels Again for the First Time* (New York: HarperCollins, 2001), 205.

the message been more uplifting, along the lines of "you are precious to God and nothing will ever change that"? Do you have trouble believing such really good news?

3

A Terrible Birthday— The Daughter of Herodias

(MARK 6:17–28; MATTHEW 14:6–11)

As a girl, I lived to dance. I was tall and willowy, my hair a rich chestnut cascade as I spun. When the Bible was read aloud for long boring stretches, I wriggled and squirmed, my toes always twitching. I waited eagerly for my favorite psalms:

> Let them praise [God's] name with dancing,
> making melody . . . with tambourine and lyre.
> (Ps 149:3)

> Praise [God] with tambourine and dance,
> praise . . . with strings and pipe! (Ps 150:4)

King David, revered among my people, danced before the Ark. If anyone ever questioned me, I'd silence them with *that*. Caught up in a filmy cocoon of swirls, arcs, and bends, I never really noticed the audience. Jingly bells at ankles and wrists, I made my own music.

In her scramble to the top, my mother had yanked me along. She guarded her grudges more closely than she protected me, and

I could never understand why she grew so tense at the mention of John the Baptist's name. She was attentive and cautious as I danced that night. I'd do whatever she asked, just to keep dancing. Her demands were simply another pull I'd grown used to. There was, I guess, a delicate dance in our relationship—until the night I held the power.

I moved with supple grace at that birthday party, pleased to be the center of attention. I bent strong as a bow and limber as a sapling. I pivoted with the vivacity of a thunderstorm. But even I was startled when Herod offered, "Ask for whatever you wish and I will give it" (Mk 6:22). Flushed and out of breath, I couldn't believe the tantalizing offer. At first I thought of silken gowns that would spill like water as I turned, or the dancing slippers I'd seen in the marketplace, the colors of the desert blooming. When I hesitated, he coaxed, "even half my kingdom!" I couldn't imagine that. I hadn't traveled far. I was totally confused about borders. So I turned to my mother, as I had all my life.

Her answer was immediate and revolting: "the head of John the Baptist," with the gruesome detail, "on a platter." How had beauty and pleasure suddenly twisted into bloody revenge? But the deadly steel in her eyes offered me no choice. Stammering, frightened, shocked, I parroted her words.

Now I'm older, but the memory of that dripping plate and the smell of that blood continue to haunt me. Those empty eyes still bore into me. The soldier brought it to *me.* It was all my fault. I thrust it at my mother as fast as I could and ran from the hall.

That party silenced the music in me; I haven't danced for a long time. But recently I heard of a teacher describing children in the marketplace calling to one another, "We played the flute for you, and you did not dance" (Mt 11:17). How interesting that he'd notice a stalemate with children playing—team one balking at team two, taunting them. From what I've heard about John, he *never* would have noticed play![1] And what of me? Have I trapped *myself*

---

[1] William Barry, *Who Do You Say I Am?* (Notre Dame, IN: Ave Maria Press, 1996), 45.

in stilling my dance? It doesn't matter to Herod or Herodias, but it matters intensely to me.

One rumor indicated that the speaker was John's cousin; I wouldn't know. But every mention of that teacher made Herod nervous. Once I overheard him muttering that this Jesus was the beheaded John, raised. Then my nightmares grew worse. Screaming, I see it all again: that disheveled hair, those staring eyes, the severed neck, and the terrible silence when all music and conversation stopped. I relived being center stage again, but not in a way I'd ever dreamed.

I've become brittle without songs surging through my veins, movement in my limbs. But I've also heard that nothing important is ever lost. Some tiny inner corner of me yearns to dance, to live. If I don't practice my art, I'm miserable. But if I do, would I endanger another innocent life? The dilemma has paralyzed me. One day I dug to the bottom of an old chest and found there the scarves and little bells. The stiff awkwardness of my fingers brushed them. Will I ever leap again?

Herodias's Daughter Today

In an era before psychologists studied the inner life, no one could have guessed the effect of such violent trauma on a young girl, manipulated by her mother. Because the woman is a pawn in power relationships, it's hard to know where Herodias stood, but it's clear she wanted John gone, fast. He had told Herod boldly and directly that it was unlawful for him to marry his brother Philip's wife. Readers know nothing of the daughter's relationship to her father, Philip. Did she miss him or feel conflicted about her mother's second marriage? Had her mother's loyalty been swayed by Herod's palaces, lavish parties, and luxuries? She didn't consider the effects that John's beheading might have on her daughter. Now we might call it the unintended consequences of blind rage or blatant self-interest.

The young dancer's attempts to process the horror are all governed by her central love of dance, which has been suppressed by a violent memory. Consequently, the story ends on an unfinished note.

She points to women today whose gutsiness may be simply surviving. Wounded by childhood trauma, abuse, or rape, it takes all their energy just to get out of bed in the morning, then endure the day. Their earliest memories are of pain. Because they were victimized, they are paralyzed. It's heartening that so many people work to help, that so many institutions are engaged in healing.

What might the lens of faith bring to such crises? One insight is that God is fungible, adaptable, able to work interchangeably with whatever faltering direction humans take. During the General's after-dinner speech in the film *Babette's Feast*, he alludes to God's endless mercy: everything, even what we rejected, is restored. We must simply await this mercy with hope and appreciate it when it comes. Cynthia Bourgeault concurs: All we've ever done, or not done, is "quietly held in an exquisite fullness, an immensity of love."[2]

Psychologists also tell us the heartening news that humans are hardwired for compassion. With help and time, Herodias's daughter might see that John's death wasn't her fault and be led to self-compassion. The insidious process of self-hatred could be interrupted, and the burden of guilt lifted. A tenacious yearning for health might finally emerge past the blockage like the growth of a resilient plant that squeaks through the cracks in the concrete. She could learn to see her own suffering as part of the deep hurt everyone carries and have enormous compassion for others. "The great proclivity of most human beings is toward healthy growth."[3]

The daughter of Herodias might be heartened to learn that the dance metaphor has been central to Christianity. An early source, the apocryphal Gospel of John, has Jesus singing to his friends

---

[2] Cynthia Bourgeault, *Mystical Hope* (Cambridge, MA: Cowley, 2001), 63–66.

[3] Theodore I. Rubin, *Compassion and Self-Hate* (New York: Touchstone, 1975), 30.

at their last supper: "Grace danceth. I would pipe. Dance ye all," and "Whoso danceth not, knoweth not what cometh to pass."[4] The Shaker song "Lord of the Dance" sings of God dancing all creation, then Jesus inviting others to join his dance, and finally his dance halting when they hung him, immobile, on the cross:

They buried my body
And they thought I'd gone,
But I am the Dance,
And I still go on.

They cut me down
And I leapt up high;
I am the life
That'll never, never die;
I'll live in you
If you'll live in me—
I am the Lord
Of the Dance, said he.

In contemporary times Mother Teresa said as she lay dying, "I know I will soon be dancing in heaven. But I wish I had danced more during my time on earth."[5]

The activist Dolores Huerta, co-founder with Cesar Chavez of the United Farm Workers of America (UFW), made astonishing gains for people who grew much of the nation's food but couldn't feed their own children. Against the formidable and entrenched power of the growers she secured better wages, working conditions, restrictions on pesticides, and disability insurance for field workers who were, for the most part, illiterate, easily replaced, and scared. On March 10, 2019, in a personal appearance at the

---

[4] W. C. Van Unnik, "A Note on the Dance of Jesus in the 'Acts of John,' *Vigiliae Christianae* 18, no. 1 (1964): 1–5.

[5] Mary Pipher, *Women Rowing North* (New York: Bloomsbury, 2019), 68.

age of eighty-eight in Oakland, California, she was asked what she might have done if she hadn't been an activist. "I'd have been a dancer," she smiled. Her interviewer responded quickly, "You've danced on the stage of justice."

Between two implacable forces—John's moral certitude, Herod's authority—emerges a third alternative. The dance is simply beautiful; it makes no claims to power. Herodias's daughter weaves between John, who speaks freely but is bound in prison, and Herod, who seems to have the final say but is fearful of the people and worried about saving his reputation in front of his guests. In between is art's pure delight.

It may not be too much of a stretch to see a similar pattern in a contemporary situation. Few places were as charged with fear, intransigence, and violence as border zones in the summer of 2019. Into the unlikely setting of the US-Mexico border two artists inserted three pink seesaws. Eli Rosenberg reports: "Virginia San Fratello, a professor at San Jose State University who designed the project with fellow architect Ronald Rael, said that the pair had made a conscious choice to combat the heavily charged politics of the border with a simple emotion: the joy of a child's playground." Their playful design brought into the arena an almost unheard sound, laughter, as people on one side played with those on the other. "The project draws power from its simplicity, the way it presented a vision of another reality at the border that contrasts with the one created by the heated immigration debate."[6] Unsurprisingly, videos of the seesaws drew millions of viewers, perhaps reflecting people's longing for something easy, healthy, concrete, and unitive.

QUESTIONS FOR REFLECTION AND DISCUSSION

1. Bearing in mind the thinking above, what future would you write for the paralyzed dancer? What ending to her story

---

[6] Eli Rosenberg, "Two Artists Built Seesaws across the US-Mexico Border," *Washington Post*, July 30, 2019.

would you create? How might she respond to the quotations in this chapter from the General and Bourgeault? How might she work her way to the line of the psalm, "You have changed my mourning into dancing" (Ps 30:11)?

2. What is your creative outlet, and what is the relationship between it and your spirituality? (Some may hesitate here, thinking they aren't a musician who performs regularly, a published author, or an artist who exhibits in galleries. But think again! Sometimes it's an art to wheedle a balky toddler, encourage a reluctant senior to get out of bed, grow tomatoes, maintain a friendship across a long distance, hike or canoe, joke with a dour neighbor, read with great pleasure, see a problem differently from everyone else, bake zucchini bread for the grieving, organize, run, delegate, plunge into a messy closet or cluttered room and leave it in order, choose colors that harmonize, fix computer problems, delight in natural beauty. Human beings are creative because we're made in the image of a marvelous Creator. What's your part of this big pie?)

3. A poignant postscript surfaces as Jesus becomes more widely known. Describing Herod's puzzlement over Jesus, wondering if the beheaded John had resurfaced to haunt him, Luke writes, "and he kept trying to see him" (Lk 9:9, NAB). Oddly, the scruffiest peasants seemed to have no trouble seeing Jesus. Why couldn't a reigning king with huge powers accomplish something so ordinary? It could mean either that Jesus did not reveal himself to Herod, or that Herod had a vision problem. How would you explain that line? Does it describe anyone you know, or any puzzled part of yourself?

4

"Heal Me Too"— Mrs. Bartimaeus

(Mark 10:46–52; Mark 8:22–26)

I was so embarrassed, I started the shushing. There, in front of everyone, my husband bellowed to some fool preacher called Jesus. Where Mark later said, "Many rebuked him," I was first. I must have told him twenty times to hush, but that only made it worse. The ridiculous man just kept broadcasting his need. Why couldn't he hide it politely, as all the rest of us had learned to do? I for one knew how to keep needs bundled, almost smothered. It was startling when Jesus stood still. How, in all the tumult and noise, had he heard one lone voice of one unimportant person on the fringe?

I must admit my outrage when some idiot in the crowd whispered, "Take courage; get up, he is calling you" (Mk 10:49). Now I was doomed—history! toast! I couldn't look when he eagerly threw aside his cloak to "spring up." The man hasn't sprung in twenty years. The last coil of energy I remember was during our courtship. Before his accident he was springy—but now he was old and awkward, so he "lurched." Was this a pathetic effort to recapture an earlier happiness? Was he crazy to think this guy might help him? And how did he ever find his way to that voice?

After he impetuously tossed the cloak, was it some homing instinct that led him to what he needed most?

It seemed so futile and heartbreaking, I started trudging home. On the way I worried about him being shamed and disappointed in front of the crowd. How would I endure their nasty gossip? In a place the size of Jericho, word gets around faster than the flip of a bird's wing. So I guess I missed the healing.

But I got the story secondhand. All the neighbors chattering eagerly at once, and then ol' Bart, himself, appearing at the door. He rushed right for me, elated, fairly leaping. For a moment I hoped he'd forgotten how much better I looked the last time he saw me. What if he noticed the weight I'd gained? The stress of those years had taken its toll on my body. I knew I was more stooped, had more gray hairs and wrinkles. But he drew me into his arms as though I were his bride. Kissing my hair, he told me how beautiful I was. Well, I won't lie. I relished that—what woman doesn't want to drink the youth potion?

Once the neighbors went home and the excitement had died down, I faced the harsh realities. Daily I worried. He made a reasonable living as a beggar; I didn't want to lose it. With his sight returned, he'd get no sympathy. Now what would we do? Was he expecting *me* to start some lucrative career? Even deeper bubbled a dark thought. For all those years I had been his eyes. Now with his sight, would he still need me? We had a *system* for coping then; now he'd wrecked it. Sometimes he stares at me so intently I want to scream.

There were no answers to the tough questions, but then I heard a similar story. I couldn't resist going to Bethsaida, where I met the sister of another blind man whom Jesus had cured. Her story was remarkably similar to mine. But in one way it was worse. Her brother's cure didn't go smoothly. There he sat, begging just for a touch, a soft hand on his aching head. This same charlatan named Jesus took him by the hand and led him outside the village. The poor rube trotted along like a dog hoping for a snack, alert, sniffing.

Well, Jesus probably took him away because he didn't want everyone seeing how botched the process was. The first time it didn't work. I can picture her brother looking up, moisture leaking from his eyes. To him, the people looked like trees! So Jesus had to try again. Imagine! He calls himself a healer and can't even get it right the first try! I laughed just hearing the story. She had no answers either and just seemed caught up in the magic of the event, poor ninny.

She babbled on about the clear pools of her brother's eyes, the amber shade of stones at the bottom of a stream. He'd once been uncertain, staying inside the dark house because sunshine didn't make any difference. Now he was striding around confidently, asking her the names of colors. She was so amazed and grateful she might even have used the word "miracle." "Well, dearie," I wanted to say. "All that wide-eyed wonder doesn't pay the bills!"

Meanwhile, back at the ranch, I'm growing used to Bartimaeus's wild enthusiasm for everything he can see. He'll run in from the garden, balancing vegetables in one hand and flowers in the other. "Look!" he'll cry with a child's delight. He never misses a sunrise, which has interrupted my sleep and made me even crabbier. Aglow himself, he watches the dawn stroke the treetops and hillsides. A walk to the market takes forever. He stops, astonished, at every bend in the road. Connecting voices with faces is another exercise in sheer glee.

When he says he's following "on the way," what does that mean? Does it have something to do with this newfound awe and praise? I feel left behind. Even the things I take for granted *stun* him. He gets eloquent about a lake glazed with the silver mesh of sun, or buds curled tight as fists. To him, every annoying insect is a marvelous toy. My husband has become as curious as my infant grandson, examining the intricacies of his own hands and toes with painstaking attention.

And don't get him started on stars or the patterns in clouds! Please! I've got dishes to wash and a porch to sweep. Part of me wishes he'd shut up, but another part wants to see everything as freshly as he does—like taking that first stroll through paradise in Genesis. Every day he's as intrigued as Adam. When do I get the chance to take his hand and look out like Eve? It sounds crazy, but I'm almost tempted to echo his words, "Master, I want to see."

MRS. BARTIMAEUS TODAY

All human beings resist change, even though it seems intrinsic to the order of the universe. Every insect, tree, and human being changes. Yet Mrs. Bartimaeus stubbornly resists. She has grown used to her blind husband's dependence on her; with his cure, their long-established roles change dramatically. It's as if their familiar world has suddenly spun out of her control.

There's often a cost to a healing, perhaps one reason Jesus asks the apparently obvious question, "Do you want to be cured?" Had he thought about the effects of the healing on those around Bartimaeus? Suddenly, his wife must give up the role she's played so long as "his eyes." It's natural for her to wonder if she'll still be needed. Perhaps for Jesus, the strong desire to restore human beings to their creator's original dream, their fullness of life, rules out any other consideration.

The healings of two blind men come close together in Mark's Gospel. It's not such a stretch to imagine the women who were surely affected by these cures comparing notes afterward. But where the wife grumbles, the sister praises. What accounts for such difference? Surely Mrs. Bartimaeus is more pragmatic—and she has legitimate questions about support and survival in a hardscrabble economy. She's similar to the Pharisees, who criticize healing when it happens on the Sabbath, breaking custom and rule. Some delicate, poetic wisp of her, however, longs to simply relax and enjoy the gift.

The sister of the other blind man sees it more positively—or perhaps she hasn't yet realized the practical aspects. The earlier story certainly has more earthy details she may have relished long afterward. John Meier says of the cure in Mark 8: "To put it as delicately as possible: having Jesus spit in a person's face does not seem to fit any stream of Christology in the early church. Moreover, nowhere else in the New Testament does Jesus' healing action fail to have its full effect immediately and therefore need to be repeated."[1]

Mark positions Bartimaeus's cure as the last miracle he records; it happens when Jesus is only fifteen miles away from Jerusalem and his passion. That placement speaks eloquently. In light of the far horizon, the culmination of his life, one annoying, shouting man on the side of the road couldn't possibly make a difference. Bartimaeus is more of a detour, an interruption of the grand schema that must be playing out in Jesus's mind.

And yet, Jesus stands still. He takes note of the individual. At the vortex of the tumult, Jesus focuses on the desperate voice. Perhaps Jesus even needs Bartimaeus's headlong response; when so many would turn away, rejecting him, this one leaped forward with massive trust. Somehow, Jesus also knew Mrs. Bartimaeus's wariness. Her story is left unfinished, but at some level he must have held her fretting self in his all-embracing care. And for both of them, he proceeded on to Calvary.

QUESTIONS FOR REFLECTION AND DISCUSSION

1. How do you handle the natural human resistance to change? How do you feel when you're not in control? Or is it more subtle—do you have favorite strategies to try to maintain control all the time?

2. With which woman—the wife or the sister—did you resonate more? Could you be a bit like both?

3. How might you respond to the words, "He is calling you"? Would you cast aside everything and rush headlong as Bartimaeus does, or stall: "Thanks. Let me just take care of a few details first"?

---

[1] John Meier, *A Marginal Jew: Rethinking the Historical Jesus*, vol. 2 (New York: Doubleday, 1994), 693.

4. If Jesus asked you, as he asked Bartimaeus, "What do you want me to do for you?" what would you answer? (Caution: the first, easy answer might not be the truest.)

5. Notice that he asks the same question of James and John immediately before he asks Bartimaeus (Mk 10:36). Their response is much more ambitious: they want seats of honor in Jesus's glory, not realizing the cost. What might be the cost or consequences of your request?

6. One of the most remarkable things about this story is how Jesus "stood still," an unmoving oasis in a swirl of activity. Have you ever interrupted your concentrated progress toward a goal to be a generous listener? If so, describe that occasion. If not, has anyone ever done that for you?

7. Turn Mrs. Bartimaeus's last words (above) into a prayer. Complete the sentence: "Master, I want to see . . . "

5

My Crazy Dad—The Daughter of Zacchaeus

(Luke 19:1–10)

My dad taught me to climb trees, and not many girls did *that* in Jericho. Sycamores were his favorite; he'd show me the knotty handholds. Once we were swaying at the top, he'd sweep the horizon with one open hand. "Box seats on the whole town, sweetie!" I'd grin back at him and feel as if I were queen of the world. From my leafy perch I ruled with kind nobility, tall and true. And he would be my king. Later, I'd appreciate his giving me a spunk my friends didn't have.

I was his only daughter, so I could wheedle, "Daddy, which dress should I get, the red or the blue?" I knew exactly what he'd say: "Aw, darlin' . . . get both!" He delighted in bringing me gifts: maybe a scarf the blue-lavender shades of the ocean, or candy from another country. I never knew how much anything cost; daddy never mentioned price. By the time I was twelve, I stood as tall as he did. We'd play like buddies together, tuning out any disapproving clucks about the bark in our hair or the scrapes on our shins.

But as I grew older, I noticed grumbling. People hated daddy's profession and his wealth. The Roman military occupation meant some people lived in constant fear of losing their livelihood or land to high taxes. Probably because they were scraping to eat regularly, we, by contrast, seemed too carefree in our high balcony of branches. But swaying there, imagining I could touch lacy clouds, I didn't much care.

Of course, Dad took me with him the day that Jesus entered town. He never wanted me to miss anything, so we ran ahead of the crowd like lookouts, gasping and flushed. I had scrambled up the tree beside dad when suddenly I glimpsed an upturned chin. Even better, the face below us was *grinning* and inviting himself to our house.

Dad scrambled down that tree, for the first time leaving me to fend for myself. Good thing I'd shinnied down trees before! I overheard Dad say something about giving to the poor, which didn't surprise me. He'd always opened his purse to just about anyone who'd ask. I couldn't complain. I'd received so many of his gifts, why not share the bounty?

Dad was usually exuberant, but with his guest alongside, he danced toward home. I was doing a little jig myself, trying to keep up and eavesdrop. My dad always enjoyed a good joke, and this fellow was matching him with riddles and stories that left them both howling. Meanwhile, the crowd kept up the criticism, pecking at Dad ("That crook!") like chickens at grain. But he wouldn't let their small-minded comments stain his joy.

Closing the door of our home firmly on the gossips outside, Dad broke out the best wine—how *else* to celebrate such an uninvited, honored guest? While he and his guest exchanged toasts, I scurried to the kitchen, dreading what I'd find. As I'd guessed, my mother was flummoxed, whispering: "No one told *me* about dinner guests! I *had* enough lamb and bread for the three of us, then unannounced, another hungry person appears at the door!"

But I liked this surprise guest, because he had the same lilting laughter as my dad. So I didn't mind helping to prepare a meal. Who *else* would run next door to borrow more food? The stranger breathed deep of the roasting fragrance and complimented *both* mom and me. To him, I wasn't the annoying kid. I was the princess who ruled with wisdom and grace. I wonder if he's also a tree climber.

Zacchaeus's Daughter Today

When religion is mistaken as grim or dour drudgery, Zacchaeus reminds us (and his daughter) with a grin: maybe it should be fun and delight. More serious sorts who like cut-and-dried answers and rigid doctrine might squelch curiosity. Their religion invites only one response: believe it or else! But for Zacchaeus and his daughter, curiosity is rewarded.

What tethers the gospel to reality is the earthy detail, in this case the sycamore tree. Trying to see Jesus, Zacchaeus climbs one. He shows all Christians who came after him that reaching for the kingdom isn't some ethereal search. Instead, human efforts are grounded and rooted in this city, this road, this particular person's gifts and limitations.

Although she caught allusions, Zacchaeus's daughter might not have known how hated her father was for colluding with the "enemy." Not only were Rome's taxes oppressive, but the occupiers also required the people to give a Roman soldier anything he wanted. Refusal meant swift, severe punishment. It's not surprising that guerrilla warfare ensued, and local revolts grew into widespread revolution against Rome in 66 CE.[1]

Jesus horrified all of Jericho by spending the night not with the local rabbi or prominent Pharisee, but with Zacchaeus, the hated tax collector. From this story Frederick Buechner expands the basic principle to include all who don't necessarily make the "most holy" lists: "God makes . . . saints out of fools and sinners because there is nothing much else to make of."[2] What a relief and encouragement!

---

[1] Carol Newsome and Sharon Ringe, eds., *The Women's Bible Commentary* (Louisville, KY: Westminster/John Knox Press, 1992), 391.

[2] Frederick Buechner, *The Faces of Jesus* (New York: Riverwood/Simon and Schuster, 1974), 100, 130.

Zacchaeus and his imagined daughter have a healthy father-daughter relationship, which might help us think about God as father. That relationship is problematic for women who've been abused by their fathers, but it stands so squarely in the tradition we might take a look. Saint Catherine of Siena imagined God calling her, "O my dearest daughter." She responded, "O eternal Father! . . . You have fallen in love with what you have made! You are pleased and delighted over her within yourself, as if you were drunk [with desire] for her salvation. She runs away from you and you go looking for her. She strays and you draw closer to her. You clothed yourself in our humanity, and nearer than that you could not have come."[3]

Interestingly, the woman who wrote this, Catherine, had to convince her dad (the father of twenty-four children!) that she didn't want to wed, as was customary, but to devote her life to Jesus and his people. Her father finally conceded that Jesus wouldn't make a bad son-in-law. Catherine went on to confront injustice, sweetly informing the pope that his court stank of sin. She had the courage to bury the dead when plague swept through her native Italy. A stubborn, blunt, outspoken taboo breaker, she must've made her papa proud. One biographer writes, "She may have been told that women were inferior, but she obviously did not believe it."[4]

Another doctor of the church who had a strong, tender relationship with her father is Thérèse of Lisieux. She described her relationship to God as a little child, sleeping fearlessly in her father's arms, hiding her face in his hair. When Thérèse was four, her mother died, and her father continued to indulge and pamper her. She credits him and her sisters in her autobiography: "I was really a child who was fondled and cared for like

---

[3] Catherine of Siena, "Dialogue 153," in Mary O'Driscoll, *Catherine of Siena* (Hyde Park, NY: New City Press, 1993), 88–89.

[4] John Kirvan, *Set Aside Every Fear* (Notre Dame, IN: Ave Maria Press, 1997), 12.

few other children on earth, especially among those deprived of their mothers."[5]

Thérèse loved her dad dearly, but when she entered Carmel at age fifteen, he developed serious mental illness. The sensitive teenager was forbidden to see him again; worse, the gossips blamed his mental collapse on her leaving home. The mature Thérèse revised her glorious concepts of martyrdom and began to see it as her gentle father, lying in a 500-bed mental hospital with a handkerchief covering his head.[6] It's quite possible he influenced her development of "the little way" that celebrates the ordinary and shows a path to holiness through the most routine, rutted, even confined circumstances.

Questions for Reflection and Discussion

1. In the end, Catherine of Siena became one of our gutsiest saints, a doctor of the church, who called the pope "sweet babu" and told him what to do. Could there be some connection between her confidence and her certainty of God as loving Father, just as the narrator (above) learns her feistiness from her dad?

2. What role do you think a father plays in a healthy woman's development? If she lacks this relationship, what are ways to compensate?

3. A way of responding to this scripture passage, or the daughter's story, is by writing a haiku. The traditional form is 5/7/5 syllables per line, but if that doesn't fit, be inventive. No one's checking. Here's a sample for starters:

Shinnying up tree.
"Today I'll come to your house."
Sliding down to grace.

---

[5] *Story of a Soul: The Autobiography of St. Thérèse of Lisieux,* 3rd ed. (Washington, DC: Institute of Carmelite Studies, 1996), 75.

[6] Patricia O'Connor, *The Inner Life of Thérèse of Lisieux* (Huntington, IN: Our Sunday Visitor, 1977), 70.

6

The Mother Who Brought Her Child to Jesus

(MARK 10:13–16; MATTHEW 18:1–5, 19:13–15)

THE MOTHER

Her father rejected Hannah the minute he knew she was a girl. We had a terrible struggle when he wanted to place her outside to die or be picked up by anyone who strolled by. She could've faced a life of slavery or horrid possibilities that I didn't want to imagine. It was a common practice; many people didn't want a female baby.[1] I've always been grateful I talked him out of *that*, but he continued to regard her as useless.

And his view is supported by the rabbis! They teach that "it is well for those whose children are male, but ill for those whose children are female. . . . At the birth of a boy all are joyful, but at the birth of a girl all are sad"—except for their mothers, sisters, aunts, and grandmothers? And yet another teaching claims that "all women are potential adulteresses unless carefully guarded and

---

[1] Carol Newsome and Sharon Ringe, eds., *The Women's Bible Commentary* (Louisville, KY: Westminster/John Knox Press, 1992), 393.

given much busywork." And the good Jewish boy prayed daily, "I thank God I am not a Gentile, an uneducated man, or a woman."

To me, she was always beautiful: toes like pink shells; the delicate arc of her shoulder; and a fuzzy head. I cradled her close and sang to her whenever he threatened to leave her out to starve. A terrible tension grew between him and me. But I loved her weight in my arms, the sweet dampness at the back of her neck after a nap. It was hard to believe that in our society, even in our home, my precious daughter counted as nothing.

Hannah grew up happy, cuddly, eagerly lifting her head to see what was new. Her radiant smile beamed like a shaft of sunlight in fog. Always, I shielded her, fearing where her curiosity might lead. Never too far away, I protected her every move. I worried that even the bright flax of her hair in sunlight might attract danger.

Then one day while we were out for our walk, her hand secure in mine, we heard a commotion. Other mothers with their children were crowding around a man. I didn't want to miss out. Could a girl come too? As I edged forward, I heard harsh words from other men trying to drive us away. I've experienced enough of that discouragement to last a lifetime, so I tried to distract Hannah and turned in another direction.

But she was stubborn, like her mother. She insisted on plunging forward to investigate. Nothing, not even my strong arms, could restrain her. Soon I heard loud indignation and feared for her safety. Astonishing, though. The speaker was rebuking his friends, inviting the children, not sending them away.

Hannah was drawn to the kind voice; I couldn't prevent her lurching toward him. The next thing I knew, she was scooped into his arms, round as a bowl. He hugged her and blessed her as I have done every day of her life. The gesture must have seemed familiar, intimate. She didn't struggle beneath his hands or wail for me as I'd expected. Instead, she cupped his chin in her tiny hand and traced his eyebrow with one plump finger.

It was tempting to tell her father, triumphant. But that night I heard Hannah humming herself to sleep, utterly content and self-contained. Maybe she didn't need that time with the teacher, but I did. The reassurance he extended to her found a home in me. I could've easily been the unsure girl who scrambled into the big hug just to hear, "You're OK." More than OK, but my words couldn't stretch large enough to hold that abundance. It was as if all the colors of sunset spilled into me, crimson and fuchsia and saffron.

I knew then that the lovely image of Hannah with the teacher was a secret to hold close to my heart. It's enough to make me feel deeply vindicated and reassured that my love is her birthright. It was almost as if he'd shown me the feminine face of God, Sophia. When I pray for Hannah now, I say to God, "as one mother to another." After that day, I've lived with confidence, a certainty I never had before. Neither she nor I was God's afterthought, an inferior species. I should've remembered our own scriptures:

> See, darkness covers the earth
> and thick darkness is over the peoples,
> but the Lord rises upon you
> and [the Lord's] glory appears over you.
> Nations will come to your light,
> and kings to the brightness of your dawn.
>
> "Lift up your eyes and look about you:
> All assemble and come to you;
> your sons come from afar,
> and your daughters are carried on the hip.
> Then you will look and be radiant,
> your heart will throb and swell with joy;
> the wealth on the seas will be brought to you,
> to you the riches of the nations will come.
> Herds of camels will cover your land,
> young camels of Midian and Ephah.
> And all from Sheba will come,
> bearing gold and incense
> and proclaiming the praise of the Lord.
>
> (Isa 60:2-6)

The ancient authors got that right: they knew the real wealth, the abiding joy was in our children: sons *and* daughters. Even better, Jesus had told Hannah the kingdom of heaven was *hers*.

THE DAUGHTER

How I used to run to my mother when I was small, knowing I'd be safe tucking myself behind her skirt, clinging to her leg, or diving into her arms. That soft haven seemed always open to me, always waiting. The other children might ridicule me, but I didn't care; she was my anchor and nest. I never questioned her abundant reassurance.

So it became part of the family narrative, told over and over, sometimes with my father's sneer, how Hannah clung to her mama. Maybe it was meant to be derogatory, but I felt proud every time I heard it. When I was tiny, I couldn't stop hugging her; even now, as an adult, I long for her arms around me.

Then a new element entered the story: the day I met the teacher. Everyone said I ran to him with the same confidence I had with my mother, sure of a welcome. I was very young, so the memory is blurry. But friends and relatives say I sidled up to him as easily as to my mother. She'd taught me whom to trust and what to look for. My instincts were spot on. The warmth of his voice, the tenderness of his hands—that memory has sustained me for years.

Even when my father shouted, raged, and flailed, trying to hit mother and me, I could escape to the refuge she had given me first, and the teacher had continued to give me. Gradually, it became a harbor hidden within, where I could close my eyes and rest for a few peaceful minutes.

I guess we all need a safe place. I built mine from a sturdy base: two people who filled my childhood with all the security I needed. There have been rough times since. Who hasn't had them? But it offsets the struggles to know there's a place where I'm always welcome, always touched with gentle courtesy.

THE MOTHER TODAY

From a twenty-first-century perspective it's hard to imagine an era in which women were so discounted. Yet, as we look around our supposedly enlightened world, we see abundant evidence of women being treated as inferior. Human trafficking (often girls as young as three sold into brothels) and rape continue as some bizarre, male prerogative goes unquestioned and unpunished. Female victims of violence try to medicate the pain with drug and alcohol addictions. Sexism continues as the norm in some businesses, cultures, and churches. The Me Too movement launched a revolution, but still the Catholic Church conceals child abuse, adamantly denies ordination and authority to women.

In *Hope Sings, So Beautiful* Christopher Pramuk recounts a story from the London *Times* of a twenty-eight-year-old Somali immigrant in Italy who gave birth beside a road while a crowd jeered and no one assisted.[2] And we in the United States and Europe consider our countries and century *enlightened*? Jesus tried to launch a change in attitude towards women that could shake the world, but we've only heard and acted in minimal ways on those first, faint rumblings.

THE DAUGHTER TODAY

Writing in the *New York Times*, columnist David Brooks described how "fear pervades our society and sets the emotional tone for our politics."[3] After 9/11, people in the United States felt vulnerable, and a series of random, unpredictable shootings only stoked their fears. Politicians then played to this fear, warning, for instance, of an "immigrant crime wave," when, in fact, many were

[2] Christopher Pramuk, *Hope Sings, So Beautiful* (Collegeville, MN: Liturgical Press, 2013), 25–26.

[3] David Brooks, "An Era Defined by Fear," *New York Times*, April 29, 2019.

only desperate, poor parents wanting to save their children's lives from violent gangs in Central America.

Fear affects vulnerable children more than we might suspect. It is hard to imagine the trauma to the millions of children around the world who are forced to leave their homes and subsequently grow up in refugee camps, dangerous places without adequate nutrition or any education. Pediatrician Nadine Burke Harris says one of the most powerful ways to mitigate such disruption is a caring adult who serves as a buffer.[4] That makes the policy of separating children at the US-Mexican border or deporting parents even more cruel. At the other extreme, children who are overprotected are poorly equipped to face risks, setbacks, or failures. They've gotten the subtle message they're incompetent; their "helicopter" parents must do everything for them.

Hannah's relationship with her mother and brief time in Jesus's welcoming arms gave her a secure emotional base. According to Jim Marion, this is where the kingdom is located: "The Kingdom of Heaven is really a metaphor for a *state of consciousness*; it is not a place you go to, but a place you *come from*. It is a whole new way of looking at the world, a transformed awareness that literally turns this world into a different place."[5]

The story also offers a welcome angle on Jesus. "It indicates that Jesus's house was a house that children ran through, ready to be scooped into an explanatory parable." He does so when his disciples are arguing over who is greatest. In response, he hugs the "exact opposite of greatness," a child who is powerless, plays no part in power-games, and is independent of adult concerns. "This child upsets the economy of eminence that has been their obsession."[6] Tiny Hannah played her part in Jesus's teaching.

---

[4] For Harris's story, see Chapter 15 of this book. Also see Nadine Burke Harris, *The Deepest Well* (Boston: Harcourt, 2018).

[5] Jim Marion, *Putting on the Mind of Christ: The Inner Work of Christian Spirituality*, 2nd ed. (Newburyport, MA: Hampton Roads, 2011).

[6] Padraig O Tuama, "In Search of the Deeper Story," *America*, September 2019.

Everyone who hears this story is a daughter or son. For some, the relationship may have been painful. But this child's story shows how coming to Jesus need not be grim, tedious, or pious. In fact, it can be as natural and fun as running into familiar arms, a ritual we see enacted daily during reunions at the world's major airports, bus depots, sea ports, and train stations. As Dorothee Soelle writes, "He teaches me an infinite, a revolutionary 'yes' which doesn't leave out anything or anybody at all."[7] Still, even in the desert, the welcoming springs of hope.

QUESTIONS FOR REFLECTION AND DISCUSSION

1. Even if you're not a biological parent, you have nurtured others, brought students, siblings, nieces, or friends to Jesus. Think now of one person you influenced for good. Touch that story to the gospel.

2. Write a letter to your daughter or granddaughter, real or imagined. If she's around and it works better, have a conversation. See how she feels about sexism in society and the church. Try to give her the assurance and affirmation Jesus must've given Hannah.

3. What words of hope do you as a woman (or thirsty human) need most now?

4. Pray Psalm 131, knowing the following is background: "If the Hebrew in v. 2 is taken in its most literal and natural sense, the speaker appears to be a woman carrying a small child. . . . She says, 'My soul is like the contented child I carry.'"[8] Does it shift your understanding or change your prayer to picture Hannah and her mother in this psalm?

5. Pray this mantra that might have been Hannah's: "We find a safe place in you."

---

[7] Dorothee Soelle, *Choosing Life* (Philadelphia: Fortress Press, 1981), 77–78.

[8] Newsome and Ringe, *The Women's Bible Commentary*, 143.

7

The Woman Who Caught the Crumbs

(Matthew 15:21–28; Mark 7:24–30)

I had to shout. Just to attract his attention in that crowd, competing with noises of braying animals and bellowing vendors, I yelled louder. It worked. He paused to hear me describe my daughter's torment. It was relief to tell him about the sleepless nights, her fevered contortions, and my black and bottomless despair. Few people wanted to hear such a sad story. For a second, hope flickered.

Then I was plunged back into the abyss. He said nothing. My last chance vanished. Friends had warned me that everyone pursued him. Every Jack and Jane had an ailment or a sick relative. Who was *I* in that vast sea of suffering? How could he possibly address all that gaping need?

Sunk in exhausted depression, I couldn't consider what must've raced through his mind: that precarious history of Israel, a tiny band of nomads meandering through a postage-stamp-sized country, their improbable survival, outgunned and surrounded by superior forces, their clinging to identity, his mission to those dear and familiar, whose scriptures he revered, whose psalms he sang and whose customs he observed. Could he brush aside all that for *me*? No wonder he was silent.

Then his friends got into the act, officiously urging him to send me away. They dismissed my cries like annoying insects, not aware that they were wrung from agony. Finally he spoke, almost to himself, as if he were stalling. He insisted on his mission—clearly defined and compassionate—to the "lost sheep of Israel."

That called for a response more powerful than shouting. Abandoning any shred of status I had left, I knelt before him, right there on the rutted path, rocks digging into my knees. My shouts reduced to a humble whisper, I asked his help. I had nowhere else to turn, and my daughter's image haunted me: the spastic jerks, the face etched with pain. I'd do whatever it took to heal her.

Totally defenseless, I cringed at his racial epithet, the worst insult ever: comparing me to *dogs*? Well, so be it; at times they're treated better than women. But from long fatigue I dragged one last spark of spunk. If it's all you've got, give me the crumbs. I don't know what prompted that. Maybe I'd existed on scraps most of my life. Maybe I'd seen how utterly ravenous a dog could be, devouring whatever tiny, forgotten piece fell to the floor.

When he looked at me, deep into my haunted eyes, it was as if he could see all the nights I'd lain awake, agonizing. Sometimes, she'd cough and moan for hours. To be honest, I sometimes yearned for sleep so desperately my need overshadowed hers. But then I'd twist back to the larger reality: she was so small, the disease so monstrous.

His response startled me; it was the first time anyone had ever called me *great*. Chattel of my father, then my husband, this was probably the first time I'd ever raised my voice. And he commended me for *sass*? I was so bewildered that I almost missed the next sentence; "Let it be done as you wish."

Did that mean her healing? He had intuited my heart's deep desire; that had to be his meaning. In that moment, expanded when I saw her cured, I knew we must always stand in hope. It felt as if I sat enthroned at a big table, chewing the whole, fat loaf.

Crumbs Today

Before this encounter with the Canaanite woman, Jesus had just come from a frustrating argument with the Pharisees over what he considers a minor point—handwashing. They have accused his disciples of breaking the tradition of the elders, a serious criticism. Mark's comment sounds as though Jesus needs introvert time: "He entered a house and did not want anyone to know he was there" (v. 24).

Jesus might still be mentally churning through that discussion when the woman confronts him. Her noisiness must be an intrusion, an interruption he doesn't welcome. Shockingly, she breaks taboos right and left. In Mark, she enters a house to visit an unrelated man, which no woman ever did uninvited. In Matthew, she creates a public scene.[1]

And yet, she steers him back to what's important. Not synagogue or rabbinical teaching, which he compares to the blind leading the blind. She thrusts into his face a reminder of one of the things humans do best: cherish their offspring. He doesn't get sidetracked by her breaking the rules, and he is that rarity, "a man who does not let his ego get in the way of admitting that he has learned something vital from a woman."[2]

The transition from heady debate into pulsing reality paralyzes him for a moment. His hesitation is rare; usually he has a more generous response to naked need. It's heartening that here he shows his similarity to most human beings: uncertain, we pause, we debate internally, and we waffle. "Many women should find this Jesus more approachable and admirable than one who never makes a mistake. . . . [And he can] graciously admit when he is outwitted."[3] May we all pivot to surety with his self-forgetful assurance!

---

[1] Reta Halteman Finger, "Testing Jesus," *Sojourners* (June 2015), 31.

[2] Finger, 31.

[3] Finger, 31.

From his own qualms he turns to focus on her. How could he have missed her, trembling in the crowd? He admits he got sidetracked by her ethnicity, inconsequential to his larger vision. Jesus has the great soul of one who can confess he's wrong; he had drawn the lines around his kingdom too tightly.

What matters is her daughter; stubborn, she will not be swayed by any objection. Eventually he too would show that same persistent fidelity to sick people. Like the woman who wouldn't quit, he carried their disease on his bleeding back to a cross that would transform and cure it.

In the intricate verbal dance that follows, both parties step out of their comfort zones. Jesus must, in minutes, rethink his whole mission, envisioning its borders larger than he ever dreamed. The woman must deftly create an approach that will set her apart from the crowd. She tries several strategies: bold shouts, humble kneeling, and urgent three-word request. What works best is clever word play: she takes his metaphor and turns it to her advantage.

He must be moved by her desperation, refusal to give up, creativity, and vulnerability. She tells him she will be satisfied with the smallness everyone else ignores, that she will eat off the floor like a dog if he'll cure her daughter. Did he recognize in her love for her child the tender, overwhelming love of God for a precious child? And if God loves humans as the prophet Hosea describes, lifting them for kisses and helping them walk like wobbly toddlers, how could Jesus deny a human love that mirrors God's? The realization must have stunned him as much as his words startled her.

And it's not just talk. The practical ramification is that *after* this encounter, *in Gentile territory,* he cured a deaf man (Mk 7:31—8:10); cured so many that the Gentiles "praised the God of Israel"; then fed four thousand people (Mt 15:29–39).[4]

Commenting on this story, Catherine of Siena writes: "And there's more." (With Jesus, isn't there *always* more?) "God wanted to show how pleased He was with her, and He wanted to give her

---

[4] Finger, 30.

trust in the Lord credit for the victory."[5] Not only does he cure the daughter, he passes on the credit to her! What prodigiously, outrageously magnanimous kind of person does that?

Meanwhile, the wily woman surfaces in a Nicholas Kristof column "Rapists Presented by Their Church as Men of God" in the *New York Times.* He points out that "the only person in the New Testament who wins an argument with Jesus is an unnamed woman who begs him to heal her daughter." Despite Jesus and the early church being open to women, they were later denied leadership roles.

Kristof points out that numerous crimes of rape and molesting have occurred in denominations that do not ordain women and that relegate them to second-class status. "'Prohibiting women from the highest ranks of formal leadership fosters a fundamentally toxic masculinity,' Jonathan L. Walton, the Plummer Professor of Christian Morals at Harvard, told me."

"'Underneath it all is this patriarchy that goes back millennia,' Serene Jones, the president of Union Theological Seminary, told me, noting the commonality of the Catholic and Southern Baptist Churches: 'They both have very masculine understandings of God, and have a structure where men are considered the closest representatives of God.'"[6]

Such a narrow view of God must sadden her, the crumb-catching woman who sparred with Jesus and held such high hopes for her daughter.

The Woman Who Caught the Crumbs

You might ask why I spoke of crumbs.
My days a trail of them, prayer beads
of desperation as I scan the dirt floor.

---

[5] Catherine of Siena, *Letters,* quoted in Carmen Acevedo Butcher, "August 25," *A Little Daily Wisdom: Christian Women Mystics* (Brewster, MA: Parclete Press, 2008).

[6] Nicholas Kristof, "Rapists Presented by Their Church as Men of God," *New York Times,* February 20, 2019.

I've harvested scraps, pitifully grateful for
kernels others ignore. Hunger can numb
a woman, make her mean. Bossiness
hardens her bread. What broke me,
finally, was seeing the grim cycle repeat in
my daughter's haggard eyes. Not her,
too! Awkward and stiff, I bend.

I never dreamt how crumbs would serve me well,
small pivots to humor, juicy dollops after
grinding need.
I who scavenged from garbage, served a
heaping plate!
With a lopsided grin, he awakens her.
Her eyes fill with merriment; she holds health
like a bouquet. Even in hunger, we break abundant
bread, chewing morsels with the relish of gourmets.
What jubilant dance we do now, my daughter and I.

QUESTIONS FOR REFLECTION AND DISCUSSION

1. Create an image in your mind (or on paper) of this spunky woman, adding details. How would she look today? Maybe wearing a wild, flashy, purple hat? Or desperate, gray and gaunt after many sleepless nights? Might she sound like women today, saying, "I pray because I'm desperate. My daughter is addicted"? Have you ever reached a low like hers? Maybe it was caused by illness—yours or another's: aching limbs, depleted energy, blurry vision, throbbing head, unsteady stomach, the cough that won't quit. What name might you give this side of your personality? In honor of the woman in the story, it might be Scrappy. When every move requires huge effort, we can barely drag ourselves out of bed or from the bottom of a heap. But the wobbly, almost drenched flame of God within still reaches wanly for healing.

That last-ditch effort can be Scrappy—the insistence that we're made for more and will persist in getting it. The theme of transformation rises again!

2. Anton Chekhov wrote in his notebook: "Women deprived of the company of men pine, men deprived of the company of women become stupid." How does this woman, and several others, keep Jesus on his toes?

3. Reflect on these words that Jesus would've known:

> Can a woman forget her nursing child,
> or show no compassion for the child of her womb?
> Even these may forget,
> yet I will not forget you. (Isa 49:15)

How do you think Jesus felt when he confronted living proof of this text, a woman who definitely did not forget her child? "But . . . " he might've protested. "She's so improbable, not even Hebrew, and noisy!" Why do you think he pivoted to help her?

4. Uncharacteristically, Jesus says nothing at first. When have you found silence and hesitation the best responses to a surprising request?

5. Have you ever stood fast, even being obnoxious like this woman? What circumstances prompted your persistence? What women do you admire on the national scene who take a bold stand?

6. The woman says, "We must stand in hope." When does fear or anxiety prevent that? What do you do to nurture hope?

7. Imagine, tell, or write the sequel, the story of the Canaanite woman's daughter, from the younger woman's viewpoint.

8

The Hint of a Mother

(Mark 9:14–29)

When he came down the mountain. I was waiting at the bottom.

And I spoke up, although I later got lost in the chaos. "Someone from the crowd"? That was me. My husband, Seth, quickly took over the public speaking, but who do you think coached him? At first I didn't really want to bother the great teacher, but I was so frustrated with his strutting disciples who couldn't do a thing but talk while my son foamed at the mouth, ground his teeth, contorted, and went rigid on the ground at their feet. How long it had dragged on: convulsions throughout his childhood, ostracism from our village, all the experiences of play and friendship enjoyed by other boys denied to him. But perhaps that long, dark story had led to this moment. For the rest of my life I'd be grateful I was there.

Seth astounded me when he blurted out, "I believe, help my unbelief!" Sometimes the surprising eloquence of that man took my breath away. But he only expressed what we both felt, and whispered sometimes, after dark. We both knew that kind of talk could get us kicked out of the synagogue, where belief should never fluctuate but always stand rigid and firm as a soldier. Our son's tragedy had dramatically changed the innocent faith we had as children. Somehow, living day in and out with his spasms and contortions had drained away our glib, sure answers. But whatever possessed Seth to spill this doubt in public?

The honesty he blurted didn't seem to bother Jesus. After he spoke, my son went still. At first, I thought that he had died. I agonized for a minute—wouldn't it be better to have him as he was, but alive? Then the gesture that wrenched my heart: Jesus took him by the hand, as I had done so often when he was small. Sometimes he'd fight that, swat my hand, growl and pull away, but this time he complied, sweetly and gracefully. It was as if a peace settled over him, the way it did when I would cover him before sleep with a soft quilt, praying that he—and I—could have some rest after his agitated day. He arose easily, and I remembered the earlier promise that lifted my heart: this demon would never bother him again.

The disciples were supposed to keep quiet about whatever happened on that mountaintop, but they must have blabbered, and gossip leaked out that there'd been some great shining. If that was true, I'll never understand what possessed Jesus, then, to come *down* the mountain, and become part of that jostling crowd where I stood, a group like any, full of disease and heartbreak, compassion and disgust, exhaustion and energy, craziness and generosity.

Although I don't know about the mountaintop, I *can* assure you that whatever happened to Jesus at the summit was close to what I experienced at the base. With my son quiet in my arms, I suddenly felt like God's beloved—as if I were radiant with God's joy. I wore the same drab clothing as always, but it seemed to have some mysterious bleached glimmer I didn't recognize. Now, I want to steep in gratitude, growing richly flavorful like tea. Not that everything got easy afterward. The crowds buzzed around us, some adoring, some just curious or incredulous, when all we wanted was time alone with our newly recovered son. Even with a cure, it's not over: the long, rough way of loving continues. *My life has changed now that my son doesn't require all my attention. I've become one of the people Mark later described:*

> As they were leaving the boat, people immediately recognized him. They scurried about the surrounding country and began to bring in the sick on mats to wherever they heard he was. Whatever villages or towns or countryside he entered, they laid the sick in the marketplaces and begged him that they might touch only the tassel on his cloak; and as many as touched it were healed. (Mk 6:53–56, NABRE)

I wanted others to experience the same ecstasy that I had. For a moment I had a sense of how much I was loved—by God, my parents, and others who've gone before, and in a radiant burst, my son. He could never express it before, but now he was hugging and crying and thanking me for the long care. So, when I thought of friends who still lay suffering in dark caverns, I wanted to pull them into the light as well. I wanted them to know how much they were loved. You'd scurry too.

Sound easy? Not really. I discovered how reluctant some were to seek healing. Some resented me for dragging them out of comfy beds, pulling or pushing them along dusty roads, stirring their hopes. I'd babble on about Jesus, but some had never heard of him; others didn't care. Sometimes, I took them all that way for nothing. But once in a while, I'd lay one where Jesus might pass, one who'd reach a tremulous hand out in profound hope for his tassel. And he or she would be cured.

Others weren't cured, but they were healed. They seemed to come to terms with their suffering and wounding, and see themselves as part of a larger picture. They still limped back along the same roads, or had to be carried, so some onlookers scoffed at them. But when they returned to their families, the people who loved them noticed a difference. Despite all the forces that seemed to diminish and defeat them, they were at home in their skins, whole as God had intended. It mystified me, but simply being near Jesus gave them a sense of themselves as being larger than their illness. It no longer defined them; they weren't its victims. Most important, they were restored to being God's beloved children.

Then it was as if I glimpsed again on his garment some bleached shining. I saw my son in them as they straightened up and walked gracefully, or lay simply, in peace. I heard later that the extraordinary man who changed our lives that day got murdered as a criminal. And I wonder if he was marking out a path for us. Much as we wanted to bail, and I often longed for respite during the terrible illness, this Jesus points the way. He could've stayed on the mountaintop in great happiness. But he came down; he entered the commotion; he held a hand. It was as if suffering in love was redeeming. Not only his; ours, too.

THE MOTHER'S PRESENCE TODAY

Throughout human history and across cultures the mountaintop has been regarded as a sacred abode of gods, far above the ordinary; in many traditions the ascent of a mountain symbolizes the spiritual journey. In the Hebrew scriptures, Moses climbs Mount Sinai after his people have escaped from Egypt. He responds to God's invitation, "Come up to me on the mountain . . . and I will give you the tablets of stone, with the law and commandments" (Ex 24:12). A cloud covers the mountain, and Moses stays within it for forty days and nights. Making a covenant with the people, God then gives him the Ten Commandments carved on stone.

But when Moses descends, bearing the tablets, the rebellious people are worshiping a golden bull; in his fury, Moses throws and breaks the tablets "at the foot of the mountain" (Ex 32:19). Eventually, God is merciful, forgives the "stiff-necked" people, and redoes the tablets, so the journey to the Promised Land can continue.

Thus, when Jesus leads three disciples "up a high mountain apart, by themselves" (Mk 9:2), his action has biblical precedent. His radiance atop the new Sinai parallels the shining on Moses's face after speaking with God, so brilliant he would cover it with a veil before the Israelites.

This ecstatic movement upward is repeated by contemporary mountain climbers. Guido Rey, an Italian who climbed the Alps, speaks of the summit as "an almost perfect form of spiritual satisfaction."[1] Theodore Winthrop, who first saw Mount Rainier in 1853, described "an image of solemn beauty, which I could thenceforth evoke whenever in the world I must have peace or die. For such emotion, years of pilgrimage were worthily spent."[2] Maurice Herzog ends his book on climbing Annapurna with a direction to return to earth revitalized: "Annapurna . . . was a treasure on which we should live the rest of our days. With this realization we turn the page: a new life begins. There are other Annapurnas in the lives of men."[3]

But Jesus descends from the pinnacle experience, as Moses did, to disappointment and frustration: both enter squabbling crowds when they descend from the heights. Both figures make the same journey—from the glory of the peak to suffering and confusion below. But what seems unique to Jesus is his focus on one face in that sea of misery. Seeing the appalling need of the (probably, in contemporary terms, epileptic) boy, the disciples can only discuss the case, impotently.

Jesus coming down from the mountain is a movement that resonates with other figures who've made the same descent. We too, must "come down," whether it's from an inspiring retreat, a hike in the high country, an idyll on the beach. The air on our return is no longer scented with pine or filled with the sound of waves. The unwashed dishes, bills, and dirty laundry may have piled up during our absence. Yet, the earthy realism of Jesus propels us back to the nitty-gritty where we must live out the gospel calling.

In the United States, Harriet Tubman became known as "Moses" because she led so many people from slavery into freedom. Like the mother whose story is told here, she experienced such exhilaration when she first escaped to Philadelphia that she wanted to share it with others. So she repeatedly made the perilous

---

[1] Guido Rey, *The Matterhorn,* trans. J.E.C. Eaton (New York: Charles Scribner's Sons, 1907), 165.

[2] Theodore Winthrop, *The Canoe and the Saddle,* 5th ed. (Boston: Ticknor and Fields, 1863), 127.

[3] Maurice Herzog, *Annapurna* (New York: Lyons Press, 1997), 317.

journey south, where slave catchers with bloodhounds mercilessly pursued her. Convinced that "God doesn't want a man to own me" or anyone else, she was one of the only women to lead a military expedition during the Civil War; the expedition freed 750 slaves in South Carolina.

The mother's experience, envisioned here, parallels that of Jesus. She never climbs a peak, but she achieves great joy. Whatever happened on the mountaintop, it motivated Peter to want to build tents for Jesus and the prophets and stay permanently. She must have been absolutely exhilarated by the cure of her son, for which she had waited, hoped, and prayed year after empty, unchanging year. Suddenly, he is restored to her, whole. It's the kind of joy few people can wrap words around, but it sings in the memory long afterward. She might not have heard Peter's words to Jesus, but they resonate in her subsequent experience: "It is good for us to be here." In different ways Jesus and the mother both hear God's boundless affirmation: "This is my beloved child." Isn't that all anyone needs to know?

Questions for Reflection and Discussion

1. Have you ever had an experience where you've said: "This was my moment. This alone would've made my life worth living"? Perhaps it was a view of stunning beauty, watching a sunrise or flowering tree, standing beside the ocean or mountains where you felt caught up in vast majesty. Maybe it was delighting in a loving gaze resting upon you or welcoming a loved one home after a long absence. At times when we feel like jumping out of our skins with happiness, we see what it means to be fully alive in God. So, too, those times when we've created something beautiful—a child, a poem, a home, a pie, a garden, a circle of friends, a piece of art—bring us hope, a preview of what's to come, the fulfillment for which we were born. Are these times simply the antechambers to a series of ever-expanding rooms, each one more beautiful?

2. After such a peak experience of overwhelming joy, beauty, fulfillment, or love, what happened? Was it hard to descend the mountain, returning to the tough reality as Jesus did?

3. When have you recognized the rare grace of being at the exact place and time where your voice or presence made a difference? Maybe it was someone coming out of surgery, and in initial grogginess, reaching for you. Maybe it was a dear friend, reluctant to admit that her son had a gay partner when she was surrounded by traditional folks who all had children "properly" married to the opposite sex—and you deflected the conversation to another topic, sparing her embarrassment. Maybe someone needed to cry because she lost the job or the husband or got the bad biopsy result, and you were there to absorb some of the first, raw pain. Maybe you stood up for teachers, striking for decent pay, or refugees, or fast-food restaurant employees demanding a higher minimum wage. Whatever the issue, you being present or writing or speaking said clearly: "This is an atrocity. This—whether it's rampant guns, children in poverty, blatant environmental destruction, exiles without homes, or sick people without healthcare—is not what God intended for God's beloved children. This assault on God's own must make God weep."

4. Do you ever feel the kind of ambivalence expressed in the phrase "I believe, help my unbelief"? If so, is the following quotation helpful? "Certainty is the sin of bigots, terrorists, and Pharisees. Compassion makes us think we may be wrong."[4]

5. Have you ever asked for healing, of yourself or another? What happened? Or have you been an instrument of healing, perhaps through your tender care of sick people?

6. Try praying using this mantra: *You took the boy's hand. Take mine.*

---

[4] Anthony de Mello, *Wellsprings* (Garden City, NY: Doubleday, 1985), 237.

9

The Stowaway in the Synagogue

(LUKE 4:14–30)

Of course, girls weren't allowed in the inner parts of the synagogue where the action was, especially that day when our town was turning out for the local boy. Throughout Nazareth the rumors had circulated over cooking fires and wells, as women hung out laundry and men gathered for long conversation. Not much happened here in this sleepy backwater, so excitement was high. I wasn't going to miss the biggest event of the year, maybe even the biggest in twenty years. All I had to do was figure out a way to sneak in and listen, unnoticed.

Pretending to be cleaning usually didn't attract much attention. The men who couldn't be bothered with sweeping or mopping assumed "someone else" would do it. They had their lofty sights on more important stuff, like whether to approve this teacher—as though they were experts and it was up to them! With a mop as my excuse and camouflage, I slipped into the fringes of the crowd that day, just close enough to eavesdrop.

The little I could hear was astonishing. The usual synagogue bombast told us how wicked we were, so I wouldn't mind missing that. But this teacher was different. I strained to catch every word, about a powerful Spirit speaking good news—not to the usual audience of wealthy men, but to the poor. That had to mean me! And a promise that blind people, like my neighbor Sarah, who was always so kind, would see? I avoided the jails in town—terrible places of iron bars, revolting smells, and somewhere lurking in the darkness, evil people. But even *they* would go free?

It unleashed a torrent of questions in my mind. Would this man who from a distance looked so ordinary, start a revolution? Everyone stared at him in a hushed silence. I longed to be my cousin Ben, to whom he'd handed the scroll. Even an attendant got near the center of this whirlwind, which began with praise for gracious words.

But then, why would he anger them? The challenge that followed—was it intended to weed out the looky-loos, those in the audience just there for a thrill to break the boredom that day? He reminded my people of those beyond Israel to whom God had been kind. The nerve of God—sending Elijah to a widow in Sidon, or Elisha bypassing all the good Jewish lepers and curing Naaman, the Syrian. I suppose we knew the stories, but we banished them to the margins, rarely ever airing them this publicly. Small and weak, we wanted assurance that *we* were the chosen people, with a special claim on God, and this teacher rubbed our noses in the fact that God had a larger view of humanity. As if God had created *all*?

Then the grumbling began, like thunder moving through distant hills, but growing louder in intensity and venom. The tide of self-righteous people that propelled Jesus out of the synagogue and toward a cliff was so strong that I got caught up in it, my mop lost in the swirl. No one seemed to notice a girl in the crowd, but I wanted to see how this would end, so I slipped along like a shadow. Something about this man, a stranger even though he spoke our dialect, was so poignant, so touching, I hated to think of him lying in a crimson puddle, hurled over the precipice edge, bones broken like kindling. He'd spoken as no one else in synagogue ever did—encouraging and honest, cutting directly to truth. On his own authority too—not relying on anyone else for credentials.

I ran along, trying to keep up, as if I could do anything to prevent that bloodthirsty mob from venting its outrage!

I was terrified of peering down that hillside, dreading the heap I'd see at the bottom. But the most amazing thing happened. How could one man survive against so many bent on his destruction? When he "vanished into their midst," I felt his shoulder brush mine. Ah—so that's where he went! Like me, he took advantage of chaos and blended in. And there in our midst, somehow, is where he belongs and where he'll always be. He left us with a mystery better than all the certain answers I'd ever heard.

Now that I'm brimming with questions, I've never felt so alive.

The Stowaway Today

Certitude is the domain of the religious or political demagogue, white nationalist, or terrorist of whatever stripe. Convinced they are right, these self-righteous bigots have done untold violence to the innocent. The narrator of this story is placed in a position between certitude and doubt, the former represented by the religious establishment of her day, the latter by the mystery of Jesus. He's made the mistake of questioning their tribalism, and their only, unthinking response is murder. The quickest way to block a question is to silence the speaker, and clearly no one wants to engage in dialogue!

She's puzzled: Why does Jesus antagonize them, especially after they had expressed such admiration, such pride in the "hometown boy"? Not only does he promise to free prisoners from jail, but he also unlocks the gates of established thought, inviting another way of seeing. Barbara Brown Taylor explains that the deeper message in this sermon at Nazareth is that "no one owns God." The people were furious because "he had taken a swing at their sense of divine privilege—and he had used their own scriptures to do it."[1] No matter how noble, self-sacrificing or even mystical

[1] Barbara Brown Taylor, *Holy Envy: Finding God in the Faith of Others* (New York: HarperCollins, 2019), 118, 117.

believers might be, if they think they fully understand God, it's simply not God.

The Syrian leper and the widow in Sidon—Jesus is always marvelously concrete and personal—show that "God has a soft spot for religious strangers, both as agents of divine blessing and recipients of divine grace—to the point that God sometimes chooses one of them over people who believe they should by all rights come first."[2] The furor that results is like the vision in Flannery O'Connor's story "Revelation" where Mrs. Turpin, an upstanding, white, self-righteous Christian sees unworthy, disreputable people lead the procession into heaven, while she, shocked, brings up the rear.

Jesus's relationship with the synagogue and organized religion was often ambivalent. Jewish purity codes would have prevented menstruating women from entering the inner circles of the temple. Although these rules varied somewhat from place to place, "the general idea that worship required purity restrictions and absentions was part and parcel of religious life. . . . [Jesus] rejected these commonly accepted restrictions that applied only to women."[3] His unfettered acceptance of women freed them—and their service would become crucial to the first Christian communities.

Young and impressionable, with little to lose, the girl has a distinct advantage: she can admire Jesus from afar, hidden in the crowd. She has no solid reputation to protect, as the leaders of the synagogue and village probably did. The unanswered questions when Jesus leaves town are tantalizing. Apparently, he has no need to tidy up the details or create closure. He makes promises, raises hope, appears to dash it, leaves his listeners violently rejecting him, or, like the narrator, wrapped in mystery.

Furthermore, Jesus's inclusion of those beyond the borders of Israel asks for a strong confidence that won't be threatened by the

---

[2] Taylor, 120.

[3] Carol Newsome and Sharon Ringe, eds., *The Women's Bible Commentary* (Louisville, KY: Westminster/John Knox Press, 1992), 396.

"other." Knowing the broad heart of Christ, says Henri Nouwen, "sets us free from our compulsion to be seen, praised, and admired and frees us for Christ, who leads us on the road of service. This experience of God's acceptance frees us from our needy self and thus creates new space where we can pay selfless attention to others."[4]

Questions for Reflection and Discussion

1. Just as the girl blends anonymously into the crowd at the synagogue, so Jesus vanishes "into their midst." How might you explain this? Was he simply ordinary in appearance, or did he have a special gift for becoming part of the people, embracing all their "warts"?
2. How was Jesus's message different from that of the religious leaders?
3. Have there been times in your life when uncertainty (like this girl's) felt more honest than certainty? If so, describe.
4. Before we get too provincial about judging the Jews here, imagine an assembly of Christian leaders, whatever branch, gathered in a holy place, wearing their robes of distinction and symbols of belonging. Then imagine some upstart telling them that Hindus, Muslims, and Buddhists know significant truth too. If this comparison no longer works, try questioning what they hold most dear based on their priorities: the primacy of the Trinity, the indissolubility of marriage, the sanctity of life from conception, or the way worship is conducted or funds disbursed. Have you hit any sore spots yet? How can we be secure enough to stop cringing and move beyond our comfort zones?
5. Jesus stirs the girl's hope that her blind neighbor might regain sight. What if this didn't happen? How might this apparent failure to fulfill a promise affect the young woman?

---

[4] Henri Nouwen, *You Are the Beloved* (New York: Convergent, 2017), 181.

6. How might her story end? When Jesus disappears, what happens to her? Was Jesus's visit to the Nazareth synagogue a mere diversion, or did he have a lasting effect on her life? Would she encounter him again? No one knows, so imagine away!

10

The Sister of the Deaf

(Mark 7:31–37)

The man never shut up. It was so infuriating, I got desperate.

But that gets ahead of the story. My brother's terrible fall as a child, the dull thud and scream, when the little boy just learning to wrap his mouth around words lost them to some indecipherable, almost inhuman rant. The pitch was enough to set my teeth on edge—high and shrieky even when he wasn't angry. But the babbling was worse, nerve-wracking even, when I tried to tune it out. No wonder—because of the blow to his head, the poor kid couldn't hear anything, had no idea how to model human speech. It was embarrassing how my parents hid him from the neighbors and all but the closest, kindest family, but then, I did it too, telling my friends I'd meet them anywhere but my home.

To be honest, I was much more focused on becoming a potter, apprenticing myself to anyone in the village who knew anything, doing grunt work just for the chance to observe and learn, fascinated by the different textures of clay, gauging its colors, feeling its heft. Ever since girlhood I'd wanted to learn that art, and the fact that it carried me away from my brother was a fringe benefit. But just when I began to feel confident and sell a few pots, my parents grew older and sicker. When they lost the energy to deal with my brother, he became my job.

The worry was all-consuming. Without his hearing, he could easily be hit by an approaching cart or get caught in the path of an angry animal. I was always on edge for danger to him. My best friends noticed the stress etched on my face. I sneaked away to my pottery when he ate or slept, and it remained my life's blood; without it, I'd grow cranky. I guess that explains why I listened closely when my aunt mentioned a healer on his way to our district. Instinctively, I grabbed my brother, dragging him, despite his angry protests, to join the crowd.

There were so many of us, a river of sad ailments swirling around this one man. How could he begin to touch all who begged him? It took enormous effort to swallow my pride and resistance, but I joined in. Imagine my shock and fear when he pulled my brother away from the crowd. Why would a deaf man need quiet? How could I ever explain to my parents if he got hurt? I agonized for several minutes until I heard a wave of people repeating the one word they overheard: *Ephphatha*! The translation was passed from one to another too: "Be opened."

Had the fall slammed his ears shut? All I could think of were the towering wooden doors of a fortress, their iron hinges. Could a frail and slender word pry them open? Apparently. Like a dam breaking, my brother's voice tore through the crowd. Running to him, I heard him speak plainly, words more welcome than rain after drought or food after long hunger. It was as if a shattered vessel had grown whole again. At first I thought I'd never tire of his clear speech. We brought him home in triumphant procession, and my parents wept for joy. The healer disappeared into all the commotion, and everyone forgot his warning to tell no one. Why, we all exploded with the news! How could you tell a child who's just gotten rare candy not to celebrate?

Even after we calmed down, that strange word, *Ephphatha,* echoed through my days. I started thinking that maybe my ears and eyes had been opened in subtler ways. Had I missed some music that had always been present? Had I been blind to the beauty of a handle that turns true or a jar's curve that mirrors the hand's exquisite arch? It still astonishes me when I see the symmetry between my work and a leaf's pattern or a stem's bend. It's as if we humans open a small door to participate in the vast urge that created the galaxies. And, of course, now I can focus, really concentrate on my pottery, knowing my brother is safe.

Still, he never shuts up. I tune him out as always, but his chatter has become more of a low trickle, a soothing sound like a watery current beneath the turning of my wheel. He's not shrieking or babbling, sometimes he praises my work and never stops talking about that man who healed him, a stranger we never saw again.

Strangely, though, that guy's got me thinking about God. I don't usually pay much attention to the holy texts, but these words made me sit up and take notice:

Shall the potter be regarded as the clay?
Shall the thing made say of its maker,
"He did not make me";
or the thing formed say of the one who formed it,
"He has no understanding"? (Isa 29:16)

Was God really as intimate with me as I was with clay, the constant reminder beneath my fingernails? When I was so sad and stressed, I thought I had to carry the burden of my family, especially my brother, all by myself. I operated under the delusion that I acted alone. "Be opened" might mean a glimpse of grace, the sense of another companion who carries us all in expert hands. My only regret is realizing so late, like a fish suddenly noticing the sea. In the last few years my hands have grown more skilled as I master my craft. But the Creator's hands hold the whole complicated world. If anyone ever teases me for working with mud, I smile and think it's not so bad. God does!

The Sister Today

First, the scholarly background: "Commercially available pottery in cities may have been produced in men's workshops. Yet there is a strong probability, based on ethnographic parallels, that village potters serving tiny local communities were women or that some pots were made by the women (though perhaps fired communally) of each household."[1] Thus, accepting the likelihood of a female potter, what is the parallel to women artists, of all stripes today? Some may not have a specific art form like sculpture or poetry, but all are called to craft their lives as works of art. Faith calls us to more than survival; it leads to the triumph of the human spirit over whatever threatens to grind it down.

For the hypothetical sister of the deaf man, her creative outlet in pottery helped her endure the grueling ordeal of her brother's deafness, and to revel in his cure. Madeleine L'Engle describes this process: "In art, either as creators or participators, we are helped to remember some of the glorious things we have forgotten, and some of the terrible things we are asked to endure, we who are children of God by adoption and grace."[2] This potter both endured the terrible deafness and celebrated the splendid cure. Through her art she could express what was beyond words. It rings true for her, as Carl Jung believed, that humans produce in art "the inner images the soul needs in order to see itself and to allow its own transformation."[3]

For artists like this potter, their art is their prayer made visible. Frederick Buechner describes this plunge into the wellspring of divine energy within: "They had to dive down deeper . . . before they were done, down into that shadowland finally of their own deepest and most secret desiring for a reality beyond any they had eyes to see. Thus, their works of art come ultimately from the same place that prayers do, from that dimension of the self

[1] Carol Newsome and Sharon Ringe, eds., *The Women's Bible Commentary* (Louisville, KY: Westminster/John Knox Press, 1992), 247.

[2] Madeleine L'Engle, *Walking on Water* (New York: North Point Press, 1980), 19.

[3] Carl Jung, quoted in Richard Rohr, *The Universal Christ: How a Forgotten Reality Can Change Everything We See, Hope for, and Believe* (New York: Convergent Books, 2019), 123.

where out of their own richest silence, they sought to commune with Silence itself."[4]

There is a direct parallel between the potter's creative work and Jesus. Humans are made in the image of an infinitely creative God. God's shaping of a life has been compared to a potter's molding clay. The potter's art lifts her out of the here and now, petty drudgery, and tough reality where many of us spend our days. It reminds her of a better, larger self. In the same way Greeks lifting their eyes to the Parthenon's white columns against a cobalt sky or medieval peasants seeing the stained glass of Notre Dame or hearing Gregorian chant were recalled to their finest selves, made not only for now but also for eternity. Beautiful music can surprise and transform us when we're mired in work or draining detail. Suddenly, we hum along. Musicians, poets, and artists participate in a laborious process to craft their finest, which mirrors God's own creation.

While these arts channel a larger grace, the ultimate creative act is living out of the truest, best self. As life forces chisel us, we come to peace with failures and co-create with God our inner realm and outer relationships. In this artistry of shaping ourselves, we seek what gives life, avoid what depletes it.

By curing the potter's brother, Jesus restored God's original dream for him—that he be whole and complete, hearing human voices, birdsong, the music of flowing water, and noises that could alert him to danger, as well as being able to speak clearly. God's creativity, seen in the Genesis account of forming the skies, seas, land, animals, and people, reaches its fullest human form in Jesus. Carrying the vision of God's intent for humans, Jesus takes action to make it a reality. He doesn't use some airy magic potion, but "spat and touched his tongue." The response—witnesses were "astounded beyond measure"—sounds the way an audience reacts to a stunning new theater, film, musical presentation or compassionate, well-ordered life.

---

[4] Frederick Buechner, *The Faces of Jesus* (New York: Riverwood/Simon and Schuster, 1974), 46–47.

QUESTION FOR REFLECTION AND DISCUSSION

1. Recall a time when art lifted you out of a difficult reality and transformed your lived experience for the better.

2. Is it a different approach to see your life as a work of art? What difficulties do you have with that perspective? What rewards do you find in it?

3. Have you ever used dance, music, sculpture, painting, or another art form to express what was beyond words? Describe how that happened.

4. Why is it so important that Jesus *touched* the deaf man (and many others) as he healed him? When have you had an experience of touch communicating more than words? As you reflect on touch, consider this quotation: "The loving touch, like music, often utters things that can't be spoken—nothing need be said, for everything is understood."[5]

---

[5] Ashley Montague, *Touching* (New York: Harper, 1986), 287.

11

The Mourner Who Lost Her Job—Marta

(MARK 5:21–24, 35–43)

I made a good living, wailing. Don't scoff. I gave voice to people's wrenching pain and haunting loneliness when they were so numb they could barely stumble through the funeral procession. What of the deep-seated sadness they couldn't tell even their closest friends? I blared it out boldly. Mourning served a healthy purpose and came from the deepest part of me. I wasn't faking it, you see. I've wrestled the old enemy, death, too; I carry the scars in my soul. I said Psalm 88 so often I knew it by heart: raw grief, not a speck of hope anywhere in it.

For my soul is full of troubles,
and my life draws near to Sheol.
I am counted among those who go down to the Pit;
I am like those who have no help,
like those forsaken among the dead,
like the slain that lie in the grave,
like those whom you remember no more,
for they are cut off from your hand.

You have put me in the depths of the Pit,
in the regions dark and deep.
Your wrath lies heavy upon me,
and you overwhelm me with all your waves.

You have caused my companions to shun me;
you have made me a thing of horror to them.
I am shut in so that I cannot escape;
my eye grows dim through sorrow. . . .
O LORD why do you cast me off?
Why do you hide your face from me?
(Ps 88:3–9, 14)

I prayed it faithfully until the day I met him, when something shifted. The corpse we mourned was a twelve-year-old girl; her parents looked crushed, as if a mountain or tall cedar had fallen on them. I knew the look.

When he silenced me, I was furious. How's a girl supposed to make a living, feed her family? I was a professional, no charlatan. Others faked it. Not I. I knew that pain on a first-name basis. My daughter died at six, even younger than this child. I'd never gotten over it, and when I wailed for this girl, I wept for her. I'd raged at God, too, using my filthiest language and cursing with my most blood-curdling expletives. How could a kind and merciful God allow such atrocities?

And how *dare* this guy tell me to stop? Had he ever lost a child? Had he endured the agony of childbirth? What could he possibly understand of my deep-rooted sorrow? Apparently, on his way here, he ignored the news that the girl was dead. What kind of insensitivity is *that*?

I got right in his face and yelled even louder with rage and ridicule. His explanation was bogus: "The child is not dead but sleeping." How we hooted and laughed at him with scorn! Wouldn't we all wish that? How dumb would we be, not to know the difference? Even worse than making his lame excuse, he put us all out.

I *did* manage to sidle up next to a window and peek in. He seemed to be taking the girl by the hand, tenderly. Didn't he know that in our world a daughter was a detested burden, not a blessing? I couldn't hear what he was saying, but his posture was full of sympathy, leaning over the bed. Meanwhile, we stood outside the house, our world overturned, not sure what was happening inside, and even more, anxious whether we'd get paid for this job.

But no worry on that score. Jairus was generous, spilling over with joy that his daughter lived. The girl restored to her parents that day opened up questions that haunted me for several years after. Why *their* daughter, not *mine*? During sleepless nights I went over and over the question in my mind, never reaching a satisfactory answer until, one day, I met him again.

It was a complete surprise. I'd gone to Jerusalem to visit my cousin, and she dragged me to a horrible scene, the path convicted criminals walked to the hill of crucifixion. I'd been angry at the guy who once disrupted my routine and my sleep, but I burst into tears at the shock of seeing him here. He might've been annoying, but I never thought he'd be carrying a cross! That's how Romans kept us in line; any revolutionary would think twice, seeing those terrible silhouettes against the sky or hearing the heart-stopping shrieks of agony. But this was a face I'd know anywhere, even with caked blood on the forehead and temples; remember, I'd been up close to it.

What he said then completely contradicted his message last time we'd met: "Do not weep for me, but weep for yourselves and your children" (Lk 23:28). What? *Now* we should weep? Was he condoning my work, affirming my natural sorrow? It was as if his sad face held all the terrible tragedies and cruelties humans have ever faced. "Yes," he seemed to be saying, "you're right to weep for that." Even worse, he said the coming destruction would make us grateful if we weren't mothers. If humans could do this to him, what worse crimes could they commit? His face was so pathetic, I believed him. And I was grateful he didn't dismiss us with a brisk head pat, saying, "Stop crying, girls."

In his bleary, unfocused eyes, glimpsed for just a minute, I read understanding. He knew exactly what I suffered when I lost my daughter. He carried that pain too, became it, held it close to his heart. I don't know why he did it, but for the first time, I felt that I wasn't grieving alone; he was with me in it.

I puzzled over that encounter for several days—until my cousin told me rumors I couldn't believe. "Remember the man we met on the way to the place called The Skull, who told us to weep for ourselves and our children? They say his friends removed his corpse. Or something strange is going on. Some people say he lives again!"

It may sound crazy, but I desperately wanted it to be true. After my long history with death, maybe someone had finally beaten it. Did that quiet man carry some stronger force? Then I remembered how he'd paid no attention to reports the girl had died but just kept walking to her side—as if he defied the grim end, tapping into some inexhaustible power no one else could see. If he'd done it for Jairus's daughter, could he do it for others? We're destined to die, right? And we all struggle with that—I as much as anyone. Death, you might say, was my profession.

But this man who spoke so softly that the crowd hushed to hear him: it was as if he called us to a larger life, a bigger wholeness, the intention of God that we should live on and on. Facing him, I felt I was up against the radiance of God that my ancestors had turned from seeing. Our Book of Exodus is full of threats and prohibitions; the terrified people kept their distance, fearing annihilation if they saw God. The Lord made it clear to Moses: "While my glory passes by I will put you in a cleft of the rock, and I will cover you with my hand until I have passed by; then I will take away my hand, and you shall see my back; but my face shall not be seen" (Ex 33:22-23).

It was frightening to question what we'd always held true, that in the long run death would always win, taking every life. Now I stood before a presence that called me beyond that cherished belief: "Yes, death is inevitable," he seemed to say. "But there's always more life. Maybe it will take a different face or form, but

God couldn't bear to let beloved children vanish. Birthed once into this life, they will enter another—which will last forever."

Did lifting that girl from her deathbed signal what was to come for all of us? Sure, she'd die again, maybe after a much fuller life—or maybe in a year or two. Interestingly, the command he gave the twelve-year-old—"Get up"—was the same verb people were using now of him. I wondered secretly, though I never said it aloud, whether a long time from now it could be used for my daughter and me too.

I won't stop mourning; it's too important to express that anguish. The people who try to stuff it seem to get even angrier and never heal. But I have a strong voice, and I could also sing in celebration—for a new baby or a wedding. This life is crazy-full of sorrow *and* joy. That guy who lifted up the girl seemed to know them both. Maybe my singing could honor my daughter—who was young and joyful—and him.

The Mourner's Lament

It takes skill to pump the crowd, get a good
wail going, raise the usual hysteria.
I'm the best in the business—not to brag—
some call me before the corpse is cold.

But that day took me by surprise,
A child, it was, an easy melancholy.
When the flutes faltered, I knew
something was wrong.

Someone silenced my best boys, my loudest widows.
One half-moan choked and hung, stillborn on the
silence—like my fist, clenched on the empty air.
"What's this?" I growled. "I need to make a living."

He didn't give a fig. "Get her something to eat,"

I overheard. Where that girl was going, no one packs
lunch.
But shrouds that should stay still as marble rumpled;
only warm contours and a shadowy hollow
remained.

All I could hope for was a big tip,
Jairus's grateful impulse to the wrong one.
The bill expires when a dark kingdom slinks
Away, driven by the pulse in a child's wrist.

MARTA TODAY

The Women's Bible Commentary suggests the women of Jerusalem were possibly professional mourners.[1] If so, it's possible that one whom Jesus had met before could reappear on his way to Calvary. While there is no equivalent in contemporary society, many authors, counselors, spiritual directors, grief groups, and psychotherapists help us voice grief and find meaning even in its depths.

Carl Jung, for instance, taught how important it is to break through the social and spiritual taboos and experience and express the darkness within us. He "knew from experience that God was not offended by any blasphemy." As a boy, he thought he was leaping into hellfire to imagine a giant turd spectacularly crashing through a new cathedral roof, shattering it and breaking the walls. But he wasn't struck by lightning for the thought; instead, he experienced relief: "So that was it! I felt an enormous, an indescribable relief. Instead of the expected damnation, grace had come upon me, and with it an unutterable bliss such as I had never known."[2]

---

[1] Carol Newsome and Sharon Ringe, eds., *The Women's Bible Commentary* (Louisville, KY: Westminster/John Knox Press, 1992), 290.

[2] Carl Jung, *Memories, Dreams, Reflections* (New York: Vintage Books, 1989), 57.

Many Christians have perhaps grown accustomed to "gentle Jesus, meek and mild," but Jung was skeptical and embarrassed about such teaching, which overlooked the mystery of God, the contradictions of God, and that "as I knew only too well, [God] could be terrible."[3] He thought humans knew far less about God than they professed, and that a more appropriate stance would be awe. Jung was convinced that he should go his own way, in solitude, learning what God wanted. "These talks with the 'Other' were my profoundest experiences: on the one hand a bloody struggle, on the other supreme ecstasy."[4] He seems to describe what the Jewish people have long called sacred debate, in which Marta valiantly engages. She is a model for plumbing the depths of her own experience to learn even the painful truths God may want to convey there.

QUESTIONS FOR REFLECTION AND DISCUSSION

1. The people who are most sensitive to crisis do something *practical* for people undergoing illness or death. They clean the house, run errands, or bring bread, soup, or cookies. Jesus shows his own practicality, totally in touch with human need, when he "told them to give her something to eat" (Mk 5:43). Remember a time when someone did something utterly practical for you in tough circumstances, or you did it for someone else.

2. Betsie ten Boom, describing her time at the Ravensbrück concentration camp under the Nazi regime in World War II, has often been quoted, but some last words to her sister Corrie seem especially relevant in this context: "There is no pit so deep that He is not deeper still. They will listen to us, because we were here."[5] Jesus could've saved people without undergoing his

---

[3] Jung, 64.

[4] Jung, 66.

[5] Corrie ten Boom, John L. Sherrill, and Elizabeth Sherrill, *The Hiding Place* (Old Tappan, NJ: Spire Books/Fleming Revell, 1971), 217.

brutal passion and death. But how was Jesus much more relevant to suffering humanity because he suffered with us?

3. Marta's sympathy for Jesus on the way to Calvary is what Frederick Buechner describes as "the face of Jesus as the face of our own secret and innermost destiny: the face of Jesus as our face."[6] Although she resented him at Jairus's home, she sees later that he bears the same sorrow as she does. Have you ever had such an abrupt change in your viewpoint or ideas on an important question? If so, describe.

4. Try Marta's approach to suffering, which is so profound that we can't begin to explain it: curse God, who is *supposed* to be a caring partner. How could a loving God let a six-year-old die? Spill out your filthiest language and gutsiest curses. God can handle it. Many of the Hebrew psalms use this tactic, for example, "You have sold your people for a trifle" (Ps 44:12) and Psalm 88, which Marta quotes above. Expressing this outrage is an act of faith that God will not reject their feelings or words.[7] The author of people's sense of fairness won't condemn them for it.

5. Jessica Mesman wrestles with the impact on her faith of thousands of abuse victims revealed by the Philadelphia grand jury and ongoing investigations of the Catholic hierarchy: "The old tropes of beauty in brokenness, wounded healers and cracks letting the light in seem pathetically thin in response to this kind of brokenness. . . . In a culture so heavily invested in denying responsibility for the pain it has caused in order to preserve itself, they seem dangerous. I fear the language of beauty has been deployed to trap us in systems of abuse."[8]

If this is true, one response might be that Jesus didn't offer any theories of suffering; he didn't propose beautiful metaphors. He suffered—starkly and profoundly—himself. A God who suffers and dies is unique to Christianity. When you think of Jesus as the

---

[6] Frederick Buechner, *The Faces of Jesus* (New York: Riverwood/Simon and Schuster, 1974), 14.

[7] *The Women's Bible Commentary*, 140.

[8] Jessica Mesman, "Deeper into Mystery," *America*, April 22, 2019.

Man of Sorrows, what do you want to say to him? How do you place your own suffering into the framework of his?

6. You may wish to reflect on, journal about, or pray with this quotation from Father Richard Rohr: "Once I know that all suffering is both our suffering and God's suffering, I can better endure and trust the desolations and disappointments that come my way."[9]

---

[9] Richard Rohr, *The Universal Christ: How a Forgotten Reality Can Change Everything We See, Hope for, and Believe* (New York: Convergent Books, 2019), 167.

12

The Woman Who Called Out

(Luke 11:27–28)

Well, he did me one better. I'd worked up my courage to give him a compliment. I knew it was risky—women who spoke up in public got dirty looks and angry shoves. Who did we think we were, anyway? Creatures with brains? In short order a few men would set us straight.

But I'd admired him for so long: his gentle way with children, how he was friends with women, not frightened by us or condescending, how he encouraged us to *think*, how he veered from the rigidity of other rabbis.

And the cures! They were always for people who needed one so desperately that they were practically blind with fear and pain. Was I the only one who saw his compassion? Or was I the only one with the courage to speak?

Where had he come from? All I could imagine was he had a mother who helped him appreciate an alternate, upside-down world, one where the sorrowing and the poor were on top, and the rich folks starved. She must've taught him the psalms, the canticle of Hannah, the finest praise of our people. Like that first psalmist, he used what was all around us—the lilies of the field and the birds of the air—to teach us. No harping away at the rules, which we'd all broken anyway. Just the treasure of being God's children, and God *delighting* in us. Can you imagine?

I don't know why or how I lifted my voice, but it seemed to spring from a place deeper in me than fear or anxiety. People around me grumbled constantly, fixated on the negative. But I wanted to affirm startling goodness, speaking with joy. The words, clear as a bugle call, flowed from my finest self; I wanted to reach out of that anonymous crowd and touch his extraordinary mother: "Blessed is the womb that bore you and the breasts that nursed you!" I belted it out, direct and intimate, then vanished, feeling it was my best effort—and it was enough.

I had probably been an unwelcome interruption as he spoke about something else. So I was stupefied when he responded to my praise: "Rather, blessed are those who hear the word of God and obey it!" What could that possibly mean? Was he suggesting that women were more than their physical equipment? Had we grown so accustomed to the way men defined us that this came as a shock? Could we be more than womb and breasts, people who listened for God's words and followed them?

At first my heart went out to his mother. I'd never intended to hurt her. Did she stand lonelier now, orphaned by his words that I had prompted? Had he just opened a door to their private space, where the riffraff would come barging in rowdily? Had he discounted her? Or maybe he had pointed to her sublime achievement, not only hearing, but also doing, knowing clearly where God called her. Maybe her heart was expansive enough to hold all us scoundrels; maybe she'd taught him that.

In my day family loyalty was strong, and those ties, if attacked, could lead to bloodshed. Was he saying that a greater loyalty to God outweighed those bonds? Could there be an intangible family, and were we all somehow in that mix with *her*? This woman I'd never met and her son I simply admired from afar have become huge influences on my life.

My family might tell you I had a big head after that brief encounter. But I see it differently. I wasn't swollen with pride.

Rather, he helped me see what we suspected was there all along. We'd heard in Isaiah:

> Do not fear, for I have redeemed you;
> I have called you by name, you are mine. (Isa 43:1)

Can't top that: God had called me God's own, special. Furthermore, God had *already* saved me; I didn't need to scrimp and sacrifice and make myself miserable. Some of my friends worry themselves sick about details of the proper observance of this or that sabbath rule. As if God cares! As though any puny effort of ours could make God love us more!

If Isaiah weren't enough, I heard more about what Jesus preached. His words trickled into conversations and slipped like cool water down a parched throat. The God of Jesus was large and expansive and never excluded anyone.

The Woman Who Called Out Today

Her story is condensed into two verses of scripture, inviting us to imagine more. Where did that voice in the crowd come from? What long, unrecorded narrative might have preceded her brief words, moving her to speak when women rarely did? And what happened to her afterward?

It's somewhat miraculous that her specifically feminine image ever got recorded in canonical scripture, and delicious to think of uncomfortable male clerics in repressed cultures proclaiming the passage to giggling junior high boys. The irrepressible feminine shimmers again!

What might have made her so bold? Perhaps she had parents like Zacchaeus, who didn't squash her ideas or dismiss a mere girl. Alternatively, she could've grown tired of being shushed and silenced all her life. Her admiration of Jesus broke all the social codes and burst forth freely because it arose from her truest self. As some theologians believe, "What we seek is what we are."[1] Jesus must've known that the goodness planted by God in *her* mirrored and shared the goodness in *himself*. So he took her seriously, responded thoughtfully—and that was really all that mattered.

Further explanation comes from scripture scholar Sandra Schneiders, IHM. In Jesus's culture a woman's identity derived from a man. Formed by that culture, the woman spoke from her experience, the only world she knew. But Jesus broadened her words: "He's saying that bearing great men is not where a woman's reality, her value, her dignity comes from. It comes from exactly the same place that the dignity of other human beings comes from—from hearing the word of God and keeping it."[2]

Fortunately, she lives on in her many daughters. She could be the patron saint for women who speak up. Those once taught solemnly that the cardinal virtue is "don't rock the boat" admire her and her tribe. She is feisty and outrageous, and though the Gospel doesn't record this detail, she probably wore a wild, flashy, sequined hat.

We don't know what prompted her, any more than we fully understand what made Rosa Parks keep her seat on the bus. Nor do we know exactly what drew her to Jesus. Was it his other healings or untraditional teachings? His reputation for compassion? But we *can* imagine her and speculate about her influence on subsequent whistleblowers.

Consider, for instance, Mary MacKillop of Australia (1842–1909). Her story begins with an insecure childhood; no one would've been surprised if she wound up in an orphanage. Her father's financial failures meant the loss of many childhood homes and constant moving with her seven siblings. But at least he educated the children. At fourteen, Mary went to work to help support the family. With two of her sisters she eventually started

---

[1] Richard Rohr, *Immortal Diamond* (San Francisco: Jossey Bass, 2013), xii.

[2] Sandra Schneiders, "God Is More Than Two Men and a Bird," interview, *US Catholic* 55, no. 5 (1990): 27.

a school in a converted six-stalled stable (cue "Away in a Manger"?) in Penola, South Australia.

In 1867, when Mary founded the Sisters of Saint Joseph of the Sacred Heart, their school was revolutionary for admitting both paying and nonpaying students. She was the first religious sister outside the cities, and the first to educate children in the far-flung regions of the Outback. With characteristic humor the Australians called the nuns the Brown Joeys, the color of their habits like the color of the local kangaroos.

Then the story gets really interesting. The audacity of the congregation being directed by an elected mother general, rather than the local bishop, caused predictable grumbling among Australian hierarchs. Worsening the situation, the sisters lived in the community, not in convents—Mary even consulted a neighbor about the fish she was trying to cook, which had crumbled. *Not* the way nuns did things then! They were supposed to be above the mundane concerns of ordinary folks.

When Mary and her sisters reported a priest who'd sexually abused children, the tension with Australian bishops hit a peak; for a time they excommunicated her. It's interesting to think how patterns of clerical pedophilia in other countries might have changed if more women—sisters, mothers, teachers, grandmothers—had known, then spoken up.

A diorama in Sydney shows the bishop railing at Mary and kicking her dramatically out on the streets. The country people saved the sisters from starvation, and Mary named those who caused this suffering her "most powerful benefactors." From a remote corner of the Australian Outback she tapped into an insight known to the world's wisdom traditions: we sometimes learn more from our "enemies" than our friends.

While the bishops' names are mercifully forgotten, Mary became Australia's first canonized saint in 2010. The Harbor Bridge in Sydney bore her name in lights, and Australians belted out their raucous Olympic cheer in the Vatican: "Aussie, Aussie, Aussie, Oi, Oi, Oi!"

As MacKillop called the church to account, so Sister Simone Campbell called the government. She is a lawyer, lobbyist, Zen practitioner, executive director of NETWORK, and the most public face of "Nuns on the Bus." In 2012, this "rolling community" began six trips around the United States to oppose the Paul Ryan budget, which drastically cut aid to those most in need. The group drew unexpected attention to the growing wealth gap and influenced changes in federal policies affecting the poor. She calls her religious community, the Sisters of Social Service, "a rabble rousing crowd." Concluding her podcast interview with Krista Tippett, she struck a note of joy: "We can lament a lot, but the other piece that I haven't really talked about—but I goof off a lot—is joy. That joy is at the heart of this journey. And if we—too often, progressives are really grim. I mean, it's not a very good advertisement. 'Come join us. We're so miserable.'"[3]

Furthermore, the only way NETWORK gained attention was when the Vatican criticized the group, a huge benefit for publicity for which they are grateful. They prayed in 2012 about how to get the word out. And then, four days later, the Vatican answered their prayer by naming their small organization in the censure of the Leadership Conference of Women Religious. As Campbell reflects, "I still can't quite believe we did it. We only had nine full-time staff at the time, and we made the whole Vatican nervous." Sudden fame. What an inadvertent gift! NETWORK's website states: "It is not enough for communities to meet the immediate needs of people at the margins of our society. The Gospel and social teachings of our Church call us to work to transform systems and structures which create injustice."

Campbell calls her lifestyle "walking willing"—"doing the best you can with all the nudges around" to move from the place of meditation to the places where people are hungry. She speaks for those less educated and articulate than herself, loudly and clearly telling the "stories of good people who are working too many jobs

---

[3] Simone Campbell, "How to Be Spiritually Bold," interview with Krista Tippett, On Being, Civil Conversations Project, June 10, 2015.

and still not getting by. Stories of college students who are carrying way too much to be able to focus on that. Stories of people who don't have the money to get the care they need and die too young."

The economic chasm has widened and racism worsened dramatically in the years of the Trump administration, underscoring the importance of what Campbell named "something that is missing, missing deeply in our nation right now: that all could be welcome." She and Paul Ryan enjoyed their sparring during the House Budget Committee, and he even defended her against criticism because she'd been censured by the Vatican: "Sister Simone is well within the teaching of the Church."[4]

In her book, *A Nun on the Bus,* Campbell writes: "This concern for those left behind by the rise of what Pope Francis calls a 'savage capitalism' is perhaps the defining mission of the church of the twentieth century, and our new millennium."[5]

So women's voices continue to ring out, even when unwelcome, with messages the powers-that-be may not want to hear. The female chorus is growing louder and stronger in the twenty-first century than it ever has before. High time, some might say. Others might accuse them of stridency. Outspoken women may use the dirty words "polite girls" avoid in public conversation, but which are apt for a filthy reality—thousands of innocent children killed by guns or the tragedy of human trafficking.

Women who speak up hand on the "outspoken" gene as if in a grand matrilineage. When truth must be told, they raise their voices, regardless of personal cost. They are not intimidated by the disapproving crowd, by attorneys' stall tactics, by brusque naysayers, or by those who preserve the corporation's reputation. They run the risk of looking foolish; they easily admit to not having "complete scientific data."

---

[4] Quoted in Krista Tippett, *Becoming Wise: An Inquiry into the Mystery and Art of Living* (New York: Penguin, 2017), 125.

[5] Simone Campbell, *A Nun on the Bus: How All of Us Can Create Hope, Change, and Community* (New York: HarperCollins, 2014), 16.

And all of us are better because of them. Without the woman who called out, we might not have heard Jesus's warm affirmation of all of us who live later than he but who still try to hear and act on his word. Without later whistleblowers, the powerful would stay arrogantly entrenched and the voiceless would sink lower on the human heap.

The process of coming to voice can be long and arduous. Women must grow confident in themselves before they dare speak. Then, perhaps, their voices carry the overtones of all those who have loved and encouraged them. Exercising those vocal cords can bring rewards. After all, Jesus took women's voices seriously and based a key teaching about inclusivity on one calling out from a crowd.

Questions for Reflection and Discussion

1. If it interests you, consider one of these questions:
    - Where did that voice in the crowd come from?
    - What long narrative might have preceded the woman's brief words, moving her to speak when women rarely did?
    - What happened to her after she spoke up?
    - What might have made her so bold?

2. What are some of the difficulties women encounter when trying to find their voices, for instance, timidity, social pressure, fear of being wrong, and so on? How are you personally doing with that process? Are you helping others find their voice?

3. Whom do you admire as an outspoken woman today?

13

Eva, the Vineyard Owner

(John 15:1–9)

The neighbor's boy, Jesus, always liked my vineyard. I remember him as a toddler, all tummy, lurching down the paths between the vines, grabbing for bright objects, the grapes that glowed like jewels. The vineyard had been in my family for generations, and I had learned from my parents the complex art of tending it. My father went through tricky shenanigans so I could keep it, not lose it to a male cousin or nephew, and I held fast.

As Jesus grew older, I taught him a few things: how to carefully plant the seeds of flowers that would discourage insects; how to support a sagging limb with a wooden stake; how to carry a pail of water to a dry area without sloshing too much; and eventually, how to prune and graft. Even the art of uprooting and transplanting echoed the exile of our people; according to his parents, Jesus too had once fled as a refugee to Egypt. I showed him how vine and branches tangle together. I teased him about finding a place where one ended and the other began—he never could. We'd admire the symmetry of ordered rows, balanced by the plume of sprouts poking roguishly out of line. He was so proud when I'd let him help, when he'd learn to identify different varietals or use a new tool. His carpentry skills passed on from his dad came in handy around my place, too.

He seemed thoughtful and serious, yet, at times, playful. When he was very small, I'd sometimes hide behind a bench or bush, and poke one arm, leg, or wriggly finger out while he squealed with delight. Later, when work was done, we'd play hide and seek among the vines. Sometimes at the end of the day, he liked to sit in my lap on the porch, relishing a story and the twilight, as clear outlines blurred into purples and grays. I even taught him the words from Isaiah, which I'd put to music so he could remember them:

A pleasant vineyard, sing about it!
I, the LORD am its keeper;
every moment I water it.
I guard it night and day
so that no one can harm it; . . .
Let it cling to me for protection,
let it make peace with me. (Isa 27:2–3, 5)

Then we'd share a big, sweet bunch of grapes, the fruit of our labors.

I expected that once Jesus became a teenager, he'd tire of me and spend more time with his friends, ogling girls. Oddly enough, though, that didn't happen. He seemed to sense I was aging and needed more help. Of course, he'd spend time with his family and friends, but he managed to visit me too, lifting heavier beams, helping to harvest in the broiling sun. I felt deeply satisfied when he remembered the earlier lessons and gently coaxed tendrils into alignment. When I thought that he'd surely leave at sunset, he still sat with me, watching the last light linger on tiny buds or happily munching "our" grapes. At such a time, I taught him Micah:

Neither shall they learn war any more;
but they shall all sit under their own vines and under
their own fig trees,
and no one shall make them afraid. (Mic 4:3–4)

Those pauses gave us confidence and renewed our energies, so we could return to work the next day.

I had always cherished our family's land and, even after a sweaty, grueling day, rejoiced in its abundance. It made me happy to see those first, tender, green leaves, and as they grew, the surge of life through their stems. How amazing that dirt, sun, water, and seed could produce such a feast for the taste, quench thirst, and lift spirits! It reassured me that God wants us to be happy and provides us with more than we could ever notice or appreciate.

It also reminded me of a passage from Isaiah that had made me sit up straight and pay attention when I first heard it. The owner who's done everything possible—clearing fields, planting choice vines, guarding the vineyard—is disheartened when all that effort yields only wild grapes. Jesus would remember that poignant lament,

> What more was there to do for my vineyard
> that I have not done in it? (Isa 5:4)

I knew how much time and energy I had lavished on my vineyard, so I could appreciate how God was heartbroken over a vineyard on which God had poured care, and it had gone wild.

Indeed, God had given us the right terrain and weather conditions, usually enough rain, and fertile soil. When so much was given, how could we complain? I didn't say much about this with other neighbors; they'd think me crazy. But that boy shared my appreciation; his first meetings with scripture focused on vineyard passages. He nodded in agreement when I said I could understand this verse because I'd lived it:

> On this mountain the Lord of hosts will make for all peoples
> a feast of rich food, a feast of well-aged wine,
> of rich food full of marrow, well-aged wines strained clear. (Isa 25:6)

We reserved our worst scorn for Jezebel, who had Naboth killed to steal his vineyard. A boy's early, clear understanding of evil was rooted here—he couldn't imagine anything more arrogant than grabbing a dear vineyard that had been in a family for centuries. Naboth must have walked those rows as we did, known the contours of his land, the fall of sun and rain, and the slant of light in different seasons. Jesus had a similar tenderness for all who cherished God's gifts, who loved them as God did, and would've fought to protect them—or maybe even died, innocent as Naboth.

After he left home as an adult, there would still be surprise visits. How my heart would leap to hear his familiar voice calling my name across the vines as he rushed through flowering mustard to my porch. I'd heard he was a successful teacher now, sometimes followed by crowds, but he was always generous with his time, listening to my updates as if I were the only one in the world. It even filtered back to me that he told a story about a vineyard, much like the one I'd told him from Isaiah. But he added a new wrinkle: the owner, trying to collect produce from tenant farmers, sent a series of slaves. Some were beaten; others killed. Finally, the owner sent his beloved son, thinking "surely they will respect my son" (Mt 21:37). Was he predicting something we didn't yet know?

I suppose I'll never fully understand what seeds I planted there. But I suspect that I was growing more than grapes.

EVA, AFTER

It's not a great leap of the imagination to think that some of Eva's grapes might have been part of the wedding celebration at Cana or might have become the wine drunk by Jesus and his friends at a last Passover meal in Jerusalem. It's even more intriguing to think that when Jesus proposed, "I am the vine; you are the branches," he might have been remembering a vineyard he knew as a boy, the tangle of thickets, the art of skillful pruning, the light on the leaves, the ruby glow of hidden fruit. His metaphor is nonhierarchical, organic, and pulsing with life. No flow charts, authority pyramids, titles or official ladders, no "branch manager" here.

Vineyards surface frequently in Jesus's teaching. Instead of focusing on rigid structures, Jesus emphasizes the very life of God pulsing through humans, renewing energy as Eva's energy was renewed by the sight of her vines swelling with life. So many different branches grafted together! They might not get along in any other setting, but they thrive there. Jesus promises that those remaining in him will yield much diverse fruit.

Then, over a cup of wine, he says, "This is my blood." It must have revolted the Jews, who considered blood ritually impure and avoided menstruating women. But Jesus insisted, despite the shock value: "My flesh is true food, my blood is true drink" (Jn 6:55). He wanted to be part of our very sinew, muscle, blood, and bone.

He looked into that cup and perhaps remembered a time for storytelling, a comfortable lap, a vineyard stretching into the sunset. He knew firsthand the vessel held a precious liquid to contain and pour out his very self. What could better represent the abundant flow of God's life? Furthermore, as he spoke the words, "This is my blood," he consecrated all the innocent blood shed: from Abel, murdered at the beginning of the Old Testament, to the victims of war in Syria or gunshots in Chicago.

Jesus liked wedding metaphors, and a wedding celebration without wine could be dull. Indeed, he portrays himself as host or bridegroom and feels sad when people decline or resist his invitation. How heartbreaking the parable in which the king extends his invitation to his son's wedding feast: "Everything is ready; come to the wedding banquet" (Mt 22:4). Clearly the preparations have been intense, the couple to be celebrated is dear, and the hope and anticipation run high. Yet, those invited ignore the invitation, return to their business, or, at worst, kill the messengers.

A sip of wine marked the last breath of Jesus's life, too. "A jar full of sour wine was standing there. So they put a sponge full of the wine on a branch of hyssop and held it to his mouth. When Jesus had received the wine, he said, 'It is finished'" (Jn 19:29–30). Even after his death, blood and water poured forth as it does when a woman gives birth.

Back to Eva, who may or may not have heard about Jesus's later words and actions. More important, this imagined woman sowed the seeds in his experience that gave rise to his metaphor of vine and branches, his teaching in John 6 about being food and drink for people, his reverence for wine, shown both at Cana and the last supper.

Surely Eva would've recognized a kindred spirit in Hildegard of Bingen (1098–1179). She, too, assumed groundbreaking roles for a woman: artist, author, composer, mystic, pharmacist, poet, preacher, theologian, scientist, doctor, and political critic. Named a saint and doctor of the church in 2012, she believed passionately in God's presence and activity in creation, as well as being a life force within. One of her guiding concepts was *viriditas*, the greening power of God, a word that combines the Latin for "green" and "truth," with connotations of vigor and freshness. While we can observe it in gardens and forests, Hildegard believed we could also cultivate it in our souls.[1]

During her seventies, Hildegard completed two medical texts that catalogued over 280 plants, cross-referenced with their healing uses. She saw humans as "living sparks" of God's love, coming from God as daylight comes from the sun. Like Eva, she thought connection with nature brings people a primordial joy. More than eight hundred years after her death, Hildegard's message rings so true that she could well be considered patroness of environmental awareness. Although she would've been appalled by the destruction to the planet, she would've cheered robustly for the efforts to save it.

---

[1] "What Is Hildegard's Viriditas," https://www.healthyhildegard.com/hildegards-viriditas.

Questions for Reflection and Discussion

1. Recall a time when you experienced abundance, as Jesus did in his boyhood when he shared grapes with Eva. Describe it in detail. Was it outdoors or in? What did you see, taste, hear, smell, and touch? Then recall a time of scarcity, when finances, health, energy, or other supplies ran low or healthy relationships were few.

Now the tricky part: Do you operate now more out of abundance (trusting that the supply of God's grace will never run out) or scarcity (fearing that you'll run short of time, money, talent, food, or whatever's at stake)? Why do you think this is? Are there legitimate reasons to account for your attitude? If so, what are they?

2. As children, many people first encounter a grim God who cares primarily about the rules. To please this punitive Father (rarely, if ever, Mother), one has to step carefully, avoid breakage, and be quiet, law abiding, and good. How does that accord with the image of Jesus, exuberant partygoer who relished wine, used it as central to his last supper, which was continued in ongoing celebrations to commemorate him, and Paul's encouragement, "Rejoice in the Lord always" (Phil 4:4)? What role does joy play in your faith tradition or personal practice? Would you consider laughter the "eighth sacrament"? How might you explain people's resistance to the joyous wedding banquet, for example, in Matthew 22:1–14?

3. Is there a place that you have cherished as Eva did her vineyard—perhaps a grandparent's home, a mountain or lakeside cabin, a favorite forest or field? If so, walk through it now in your imagination. Experts on neuroscience tell us that such savoring is healthy for the brain, so treasure that place again mentally, even if you may never again see it physically.

4. In the Christian tradition certain rocks, mountains, shrines, and wells are considered holy. Place can be a "fifth gospel." Could we broaden the concept to other places especially

sacred to women, like the labor and delivery room, the kitchen, garden, bedroom, or porch? What place would you hold sacred?

5. What is your relationship with nature? Does the question make you cringe with embarrassment, protesting, "I don't have time to get outside!"? Or is your connection with the natural world a life-giving source so important that you'd never neglect it? Broadening to the larger arena, what is the state of environmental awareness in your community? What efforts do you praise and support? What regrets do you have about the health of the planet we're passing on to our children?

14

Barabbas's Lover

(Mark 15:6–15; Matthew 27:15–26; Luke 23:18–25)

Barabbas had always been angry, furious with one thing or another, but the edges have cooled around that seething cauldron. You won't believe how the softening happened.

I thought I'd never see my love again. He'd finally done it, one too many clever tricks on the Romans, and they'd come smashing down on him with all the might of their steel swords. He'd been imprisoned, and they were efficient; no dilly-dallying before they'd put him to death.

As a child, Barabbas must have been eager to please. I saw glimmers of that when we first met; I guess he wanted to impress me. That urge surfaced again with our child; he wanted to be a good dad. But in Barabbas's world, that instinct could turn violent. He'd rage about any threat he perceived to our family and vow to murder anyone who looked crosswise at us. His contempt for the Roman occupiers was so fierce that I'd try to steer him away when we'd see a soldier in the street.

You're probably wondering why I'd be attracted to a notorious criminal. Maybe I admired his courage, bluster, and utter disdain for the Roman conquerors. We both hated those centurions with a passion: he because they'd killed his brother, another Zealot; and I because of how hideously they'd humiliated my mother. Barabbas would be so proud after a successful skirmish that I didn't have the heart to question exactly what he'd done. We didn't move in the polite social circles of marriages, synagogues, and taxpayers, but our friends would cheer each exploit, then plot the next one.

I had always been short and shy, but when Barabbas loomed beside me, tall and powerful, I felt like I grew a couple inches. I was nobody, but with him and his friends, I was somebody. Our reasoning was simple: What are the lives of a couple centurions compared to the thousands of lives they've stolen from our people? We wanted to send a strong message: Go away. Give us back our own country. So what if one Roman family grieves, when so many Hebrew families mourn? His escapades convinced me to believe that when you're always being hurt, it feels oddly powerful to turn it around and become the one who does the hurting.

Deprived of so much as a child, I'd bloom with pride when he got a lick in against that unjust force that treated us like scum. If you've been cowed and frightened all your life, dreading the knock in the middle of the night or the encounter in the marketplace, you glom onto any heroic resistance you can find. Because he was my hero, I followed the crowds that ominous day, knowing that at festival it was customary to release one prisoner.

It was hard to hear Pilate, so I scrambled toward the front. It surprised me that both prisoners were named Jesus. It's a fairly common name here, but one was *my* Barabbas; the other, Pilate said, "called the Messiah." What did that mean? My Jesus Barabbas's name meant "son of the father." To whom did this other man belong? I looked around to see if his family might be here too, alongside me, but people were hard to identify in the chaos, all that pushing and screaming.

It was strange how that other prisoner stood silent and sad as the crowds bellowed and raged. In that condemned man I recognized humiliation, voicelessness, powerlessness to stop the mob—I sympathized, because that helplessness had been my whole life. They didn't get much relief or holiday, these shouting folks, so when the chance arose, they went wild, carrying on like hooligans. A swish of religious robes moved among them, almost as if temple leaders were inciting a riot—curious.

I was growing hot and tired when the rumble began. Pilate was embarrassed, caught in the middle, wanting only to keep his job. I'd heard plenty of whispered conversations among our friends who knew the enemy. We all knew Emperor Tiberius would remove Pilate for mistreating a provincial but also wouldn't tolerate treason. Weighing his options, I thought sure Pilate would release the other prisoner named Jesus. Pilate seemed to favor this "Messiah," and I often wonder, did that quiet man for a split second glimpse freedom like an open field? Did Pilate dangle hope before him, as he looked beyond the chaos, hoping briefly for a future? Any of us would have grasped at that straw and been devastated at its crumbling.

But then the fragile shimmer of hope must've vanished, as the Sadducees got busy, inciting the people. The cry grew like distant thunder, "Give us Barabbas!" How did they know his name, my beloved? Did he mean anything to them, or were they using him to get at the other fellow?

God forgive me, but I couldn't join in the chant. It was so bloodthirsty, so heedless of the one who would be doomed if my lover was released. For years I'd whispered Barabbas's name gently, making love. I'd called it out, desperate for help, trusting he'd always respond. But I couldn't bring myself to scream it murderously in public. They didn't care about him one bit; they just wanted to doom the other guy. I can't shake that image of the one whose fate rested in the hands of a two-bit, tinny dictator and a mindless mob. He seemed contained, secure, almost forgiving. Who *does* that, surrounded by brutality? I felt torn.

So Pilate released Barabbas. But to what? To me, I guess. By the time he got home that night, he was still shaking. If I hadn't been holding the baby, I would've fallen to the floor with relief. If he'd been executed, how would I have supported us? That question could be answered with a smirk, but I dreaded the obvious, a life of prostitution. My family had rejected me long ago; I had nowhere to turn, and now, a child to feed.

They gave us back our life, that strange combination of a vacillating governor, Sadducees who whipped the crowd into a frenzy, and a bunch of people who just liked shouting and didn't much care which name they spat out. At first, we touched each other reverently, cautious about believing such marvelous good luck. Barabbas held tight to me and our baby because in prison he had thought he'd never see us again.

Barabbas was scared by his narrow escape and didn't want to be in the same pickle again. He even turned away when his friends came round with new ideas for revolution. "I got off once," he explained, "but how often could I get freed like that? Pilate would remember if I came before him again." We talked later about other ways to resist the Romans. I began to see how callous it was to assume *they* didn't have wives and children awaiting their return as eagerly as we had. Yet, how could we sleep at night if we didn't play some small part in removing them? It was a terrible struggle, one we never resolved.

Now, I get caught in details as I did before: what we're to eat or drink; how to pay for the few items that keep our household running; and how best to care for the child. But then I try to pause and remember that we wouldn't be here at all if it weren't for that other Jesus. I feel a wave of gratitude that, I must admit, grows fainter as we grow farther from the experience. How to hold onto that first elation, that precious, freeing gift?

Barabbas's Lover Today

It's possible to respond to this imagined woman in two ways: one personal; the other political.

Personal

Her final question has probably occurred to anyone who has had a "peak experience": how to remain grateful even when the emotional high wears off; how to treasure that unique happening so it stays vivid and fresh in memory. Perhaps our experience isn't as dramatic as hers, but we might suddenly feel held, rescued, or part of a larger whole. We see great beauty, and knowing that it will fade, we take photographs, save a shell, an autumn leaf, a dried flower, a pebble, or buy a souvenir. Unrealistic as it is, we want to stop time and stay in that exalted space forever. The poet, Ross Gay, captures the dilemma:

What do you think
this singing and shuddering is,
what this screaming and reaching and dancing
and crying is, other than loving
what every second goes away?[1]

At the same time, we don't want to sacrifice the present because we're living in the past. Rather than attaching to one fine memory or placing our whole identity there, we want to remember that God is always active, never withholds the grace that Fr. Richard Rohr defines as "what God does to keep all things he has made in love and alive—forever."[2]

Barabbas, and by extension, his family was one of the first that Jesus saved. It's intriguing that both men had the same first name, a detail found only in Matthew. The common name is the reason Pilate must differentiate with the phrase "who is called the Messiah." Did the shared name indicate Jesus's shared identity with *all* humanity, even a murderer? Did it reveal his large embrace of *everyone*? Jesus had referred to God as "Abba," or Daddy, and the murderer's name is "son of the father"—one innocent and the other guilty; both God's beloved sons.

---

[1] Ross Gay, "Catalog of Unabashed Gratitude," *Catalog of Unabashed Gratitude* (Pittsburgh: University of Pittsburgh Press, 2015), 93.

[2] Richard Rohr, *Immortal Diamond: Searching for Our True Self* (San Francisco: Jossey-Bass, 2013), xx.

POLITICAL

Throughout history oppressive regimes have exchanged lives as callously as cloth. Saint Maximilian Kolbe, a Polish Franciscan imprisoned at Auschwitz, was lined up with the other inmates of his cell block. They were told that since one prisoner had escaped, the Nazis would retaliate on ten others, who'd be starved to death underground. One of those selected cried out as Barabbas could've: "My wife and children! I'll never see them again!" Kolbe then stepped forward and took his place. The man who was spared was present for Kolbe's canonization forty-one years later. Such stories show how Jesus's action has continued throughout the centuries. A less glorious example, but a similar exchange of life: the parents who have borne suffering so their children didn't have to.

Jesus the Christ also resolved the dilemma of whether to resist or ignore the Roman oppression. Human evolution has conditioned us for fight or flight. Over the centuries those have been the most common responses to injustice. According to scripture scholar Walter Wink, Jesus proposed an alternative, a third way: creative nonviolent resistance. This approach proved ultimately effective for Gandhi's resistance to British rule in India and Martin Luther King Jr.'s civil rights movement in the United States. Wink writes:

> Jesus reveals a way to fight evil with all our power without being transformed into the very evil we fight. It is a way—the only way possible—of not becoming what we hate. . . . Jesus abhors both passivity and violence. Why, then, does he counsel those already humiliated people to turn the other cheek? Because this action robs the oppressor of the power to humiliate. The person who turns the other cheek is saying, in effect, "Try again. Your first blow failed to achieve its intended effect. I deny you the power to humiliate me. I am a human being just like you. Your status does not alter that fact. You cannot demean me."[3]

---

[3] Walter Wink, *Engaging the Powers: Discernment and Resistance in a World of Domination* (Minneapolis: Augsburg Fortress, 1992), 175–76.

After his first visit to South Africa in the early 1980s, Wink wrote a book, later published as *Jesus and Nonviolence: A Third Way*, which offered Christians nonviolent tactics to defeat apartheid.[4] He writes:

> Love of enemies is the recognition that the enemy, too, is a child of God. The enemy too believes he or she is in the right, and fears us because we represent a threat against his or her values, lifestyle, or affluence. When we demonize our enemies, calling them names and identifying them with absolute evil, we deny that they have that of God within them that makes transformation possible. Instead we play God. We write them out of the Book of Life. We conclude that our enemy has drifted beyond the redemptive hand of God.[5]

All this scholarship and historical activity would have baffled Barabbas and his lover, who were uneducated people on the fringe. But they might've been pleased to learn there was a third way to defeat the Roman occupation. They might have been even happier to know that it was proposed by the man who exchanged his life for theirs.

Many women have subsequently utilized creative nonviolence. One contemporary who stands out is Leymah Gbowee, winner of the 2011 Nobel Peace Prize. She may be best known through the documentary film "Pray the Devil Back to Hell." She was tired of civil war, child soldiers, and countless unnecessary deaths in her native country, Liberia. With fellow Christians, in an unprecedented coalition with Muslim women, she led thousands in

> public protests that forced Liberia's ruthless then-President Charles Taylor to meet with them and . . . take part in formal peace talks. . . . When the talks seemed stalled, Leymah

---

[4] John Dear, "Walter Wink, Our Best Teacher of Christian Nonviolence," *National Catholic Reporter*, May 29, 2012.

[5] Walter Wink, *Jesus and Nonviolence: A Third Way* (Minneapolis: Augsburg Fortress, 2003), 59.

> and nearly 200 women formed a human barricade to prevent Taylor's representatives and the rebel warlords from leaving the meeting hall for food or any other reason until, the women demanded, the men reached a peace agreement.
>
> When security forces attempted to arrest Leymah, she displayed tactical brilliance in threatening to disrobe—an act that, according to traditional beliefs, would have brought a curse of terrible misfortune upon the men.[6]

Her nonviolent ruse was successful—Taylor was forced into exile, Liberia's fourteen-year civil war ended, and President Ellen Johnson Sirleaf, another Nobel Peace Prize winner, was elected. The mother of six, Gbowee continues to address the terrible vulnerability of women and children during war and to work nonviolently for peace.

QUESTIONS FOR REFLECTION AND DISCUSSION

1. Do you think women identify especially with Jesus's passion because, like the narrator, they see in him their own vulnerability?

2. Does anything in your experience parallel the remarkable exchange of Jesus's life for that of Barabbas? If so, how does that help you understand the gift Jesus gave? If not, how do you think Barabbas and his lover felt in being given a second chance at life?

3. The passion narrative is so familiar, we rarely think of alternatives. But imagine for a moment that Pilate had released Jesus, "called the Messiah." What might have happened then? Would it have been completely counter to Jesus's mission if he returned to a quiet life? Would he have looked out for Barabbas's family then?

4. What do you think of Jesus's "third way," neither fight nor flight but creative nonviolence? Where have you seen it used effectively? Where do you think it might not work?

---

[6] "Leymah Gbowee—Biographical," https://www.nobelprize.org/prizes/peace/2011/gbowee/biographical.

15

And Still, Women Wait; Women Act—Salome

(MARK 16:1–2; JOHN 20:1–18)

I'd always teased my friend Mary Magdalene about her stubbornness, but surprisingly, it became her strength. When everyone else had just about given up on Jesus, she stayed firm. Maybe she held fast, tenaciously, to hope. She wouldn't even abandon his *tomb.* So Jesus had once wept outside the tomb of Lazarus, and called him by name, as he would later call Mary. But I didn't remember that immediately; there was too much to be done right after his death.

Despite a numbing sense of defeat, a small group of friends agreed to do what we could. Jesus had been so extravagantly good to us, we wanted to honor him in death. Mark said of us later: "There were also women looking on from afar" (Mk 15:40). Even our distant view was the only direct record. The men had fled; our spare account and witness was all that remained. But no one could adequately capture the tragedy and futility of it all. We looked on and stayed afar because there was absolutely nothing we could do. What chance did a few unarmed women have against the Roman army? I've never felt so frustrated. It was monstrous; it was horrific; we couldn't possibly stop it. Even worse, were we so far off that he couldn't see us, his eyes clouded by sweat, blood, and pain? Did he know that anyone stayed faithful? Would that have comforted him?

We had no answers that blurry, paralyzing day, but it helped afterward to plan an action, to do *something* when the Sabbath ended. We certainly didn't ask anyone's permission; we liked taking initiative. As we carried our sweet spices to the burial place, we debated a formidable problem: who would roll away the massive boulder blocking the entrance? We never resolved that problem; we just kept trudging. We could've stayed paralyzed by sorrow, fear, or doubt, but it seemed important to keep moving. Surprisingly, the problem we imagined was altogether different from the one that actually presented itself. The stone was gone; only a dark hole remained in its place.

We were so frightened we could barely hear the voice that told us not to be alarmed. Most of us stumbled away in terror, but Mary remained. The story has, of course, been told different ways. Mark thought the angels announced the good news to us; brilliant information, but information nonetheless. John recorded the experience of personal, loving recognition that Mary had confided to us, her closest friends. Mary responded to her name, "Mariam," in that welcome voice of intimate, familiar Aramaic: "Rabbouni," their first language.[1]

No wonder he went to her first, without hesitation. Just as she had anointed him before his passion, now she waited to bless his death with fragrance. She had been faithful throughout his ordeal, and we had been her support system. All of us, despite the brutality and outrage of the ordeal, were held in a deeper love. No matter what's happened since, it's taught me to look for hints of a larger perspective on what at first seems disastrous.

And what about that stubbornness I mentioned earlier? Still she insists: we will rise again. Because we'd been friends so long, I believed her. But even more, I believed in the strength of Jesus's

---

[1] Demetrius Dumm, *A Mystical Portrait of Jesus* (Collegeville, MN: Liturgical Press, 2001), 38–39.

promise. Despite all evidence to the contrary, we, with Jesus, resurrect.

Salome and Friends Today

Christ, risen from his sepulcher at last,
Appeared to women first
So that the news would travel very fast.[2]

"The Apostles and disciples find it harder to believe in the Risen Christ. . . . Not the women, however!"[3]

Two women sit cross-legged on a short, sculpted finger of rock extending into the Pacific Ocean. It's early in the morning. Their hands rest lightly on their knees as the waves crash below and the sun highlights the white foam, the glittering curl. They do not speak; they seem to meditate as the sun advances from the east.

Their posture recalls Mary Magdalene, waiting outside the tomb. She has discovered the boulder that had been rolled away and the stunning emptiness within. Readers of John's Gospel do not know her thoughts, only her posture. Why does she remain when Peter and the beloved disciple return home? Her persistence is clear: Mary stayed "weeping outside the tomb" (Jn 20:11).

Did she have a glimmer of hope—a faint suspicion based on her friendship with Jesus—that the story wasn't quite over? How much did she share with her closest friends who accompanied her? Did her intimacy with him suggest surprises still lay ahead, despite the heavy clunk of the stone, the finality of soldiers sealing it? Did her curiosity trump her fear?

Or perhaps, she was simply tired, too emotionally exhausted to think of the next step. When the future is unclear, it's wise

---

[2] Filippo Pananti, "Epigram VII," in Robert Atwan et al., *Divine Inspiration: The Life of Jesus in World Poetry* (New York: Oxford University Press, 1998), 541.

[3] Pope Francis, "General Audience, April 3, 2013," quoted in James Martin, *Jesus* (New York: HarperCollins, 2014), 402.

to plop into the present until a direction emerges. Maybe she is completely depleted, but she knows deeper than language that the God who has been faithful before will be faithful again; God won't abandon her now. No matter how bleak the picture seems, she waits with silent intention; something will change.

Many women still wait and weep. On a global scale, they wait for equality, for the end of human trafficking, for food and clean water to give their children, for humanity to stop using war and violence to solve its problems. In the United States they weep for victims, often their children, of rampant guns, and they wait for saner gun safety measures. Jesus changed the old male-female dynamic of domination and subordination by greeting women as his friends, by engaging in conversations where he learned from women. But the crusty domination model still persists centuries later in many sectors. How long must women wait for change?

On a personal level women wait for the raise that goes to male coworkers but not to them, for the end of sexual harassment in a workplace they dread entering, for the cures to terrible diseases that ravage their families, for humane immigration policy that won't separate parents and children. Surely, the mother risking her life for her child, to emigrate and escape terrible violence and poverty, is a vivid, current example of Jesus risking everything for humanity. Women, like those who watched Jesus's passion from afar, unable to intervene, feel frustrated and powerless when their best efforts still fail to produce change in entrenched establishments.

The litany is long, but the women who wait take their places in honored company. Mary Magdalene's waiting was rewarded: she heard a familiar voice softly speak her name and ask gently why she wept.

Sometimes women act, and the world has seen a wave of changes as a result. A few examples in a list that could be expanded hundreds of times over include tree planting in Africa; women's small businesses in developing nations; medical research and treatment; gaining equal pay for female athletes; vocal protests against the rape culture of India; exposing predatory men through the Me Too movement; the hard, essential work of building environmental awareness; and heartening attempts to align the world more closely with God's original vision, in which justice and peace flourish.

Jesus dramatically changed "women's work" (endlessly repeated drudgery) when he washed feet and hosted the last supper, assuming traditional female roles. He transformed their status when he sent them to tell the men the good news of his resurrection, even when women weren't recognized as legal witnesses in court. Symbolically, Salome and her friends leave their spice jars in the dust at the tomb, just as the Samaritan woman abandoned her water jug to spread the good news in her village. They are called to a spiritual mission much greater than physical tasks.

Scripture scholar Marie-Eloise Rosenblatt comments:

> The possibility of a reality other than death acts as a "jump-start" inside them, charging them with an eruption of emotional energy. . . . Their "movability" and being in transit contrasts with the eleven who sit inside a room. The eleven maintain their immovability, both of location and mind. Nothing moves them until Jesus himself comes to them. . . . The narrative suggests that Jesus discloses himself very readily to people who are on the move, notably the women who have left their accustomed domestic positions which provide them a measure of protection and safety, and also social invisibility.[4]

Two contemporary examples of women on the move, representatives of a much vaster field who continue Salome's tradition, follow.

---

[4] Marie-Eloise Rosenblatt, "Women in the Passion and Resurrection Narratives," in *The Way Supplement* 74 (Summer 1992): 47–48.

Adverse childhood experiences (ACEs) such as abuse, neglect, mental illness in the household, loss of caregiver, homelessness, and bullying have long been known as toxic to the developing child. But no one understood the full effects and possibilities for healing before Dr. Nadine Burke Harris entered the scene. Harris, a pediatrician with a master's degree in public health from Harvard, working in a rough neighborhood of San Francisco, implemented basic care where there had been only one doctor for over ten thousand children.

But she was puzzled. Why did that community, where she saw marvelous families struggling mightily, have such a dramatically reduced life expectancy? Why was a child raised in that community two and a half times more likely to develop pneumonia than a child in a wealthier area and six times as likely to develop asthma? Why would serious health problems plague these children into adulthood? In *The Deepest Well* she eloquently describes distress over her patients: "At the beginning, they are equal, these beautiful bundles of potential, and knowing that they won't always be is enough to break your heart."[5]

Most people know that the human stress response has helped the species survive, cuing the first people to run when the lion roared. Cortisol helped the body by increasing blood sugar so the brain could think and inhibiting growth and reproduction during food shortages. But children exposed to high doses of stress have "overloaded systems," which can cause long-range health problems and significantly shorter life spans.

With the sheer delight of learning something useful, Dr. Harris found exhaustive research, done in 1998, linking ACEs to the leading causes of death in adults. Identifying the stress-response system as the cause of "a devastating medical trajectory . . . opened up a huge runway for change."[6] Medical terms, but a resurrection theme! Children who experience prolonged adversity and terrifying situations have a deregulated, near-constant blast of

---

[5] Nadine Burke Harris, *The Deepest Well* (Boston: Harcourt, 2018), 14.

[6] Harris, 26.

cortisol or, in Harris's metaphor, a broken stress thermostat, and the brain shows measurable alterations. The best intervention? An adult caregiver who serves as a buffer and, in many cases, needs therapy as well.

With high energy Harris relates how she and her team created an ACE screening (which she hopes every doctor will require for every routine physical). They learned how effective it was to talk about the trauma, even with very young children, to avoid their creating an explanation that blamed themselves. The best therapy treats parent and child as a team. This treatment has had a tremendous effect—as did other interventions Harris explains—mindfulness, sleep, exercise, nutrition, and healthy relationships. She demonstrates joyfully that scientific detectives can make enormous improvements in people's lives, especially those who need it most.

Harris's work is based on painful personal experiences. With a schizophrenic mother, she never knew if she'd come home to "happy mommy" or "scary mommy." She pleads for a conversation on ACEs and the courage to implement change. Harris is not only brilliant and heroic but grounded in reality: the daughter of a Jamaican doctor and mother of four boys. She contributes a splendid voice toward efforts for a more just and healthy world.

Another example, noted here because it's not related to politics in any way and isn't controversial, concerns the first all-female crew to sail successfully around the world in 1989–90. The film version, *Maiden* (titled after the name of their boat), begins with the sad story of a ten-year-old girl named Tracy Edwards, whose happy childhood crashed to an end when her father died. The man her mother later married was abusive and alcoholic. Tracy was suspended from secondary school many times before she was finally expelled at sixteen. She ran away from home, became a nomad, and worked on boats as the cook.

During one of her odd jobs she met King Hussein of Jordan, who became a close friend and would later fund her boat and historic voyage. Edwards faced intense sexism and plenty of people who said it couldn't be done, including a *Guardian* yachting reporter who called her crew "a tinful of tarts."[7] The skepticism of male critics echoes what Salome and her friends encountered with male disciples: a refusal to see things might be different from the established order, a quick dismissal of female initiative.

But the international crew of fourteen women won two legs, including the most treacherous, of the Whitbread Round the World Race, thirty-two-thousand nautical miles from England to Uruguay to Australia to New Zealand and back, with a stop in America. Edwards became the first woman in Whitbread history to be named Yachtsman of the Year. When the yacht came into Fremantle, Edwards recalled, "the collective jaws around the world just dropped."[8] In characteristically dry British style, some of their male competitors and critics simply commented, "Blimey!"

To film director Alex Holmes's delight, archival footage of the 1989 race existed; Whitbread organizers had asked for volunteers to film themselves during the race. Edwards agreed, recalling: "If we triumph, this is a record for any woman who comes after us." The unseen epilogue, after the highs and lows of the film crashing like waves, was Edwards's struggle with depression, her mother's illness, and her own most human difficulties.

The mature woman speaks now of her commitment to "creating visibility—about what women are capable of, about mental health, about what's possible when you put together the right team."[9] Thirty years later her daughter, Mack Edwards-Mair,

---

[7] Writer Michael Schulman recounts Edwards's response: "When we came first in New Zealand, he [Bob Fisher] wrote, 'They're not just a tinful of tarts. They're a tinful of smart, fast tarts.' Which we loved, until someone pointed out the word 'tart' is still in there" (Michael Schulman, "How Tracy Edwards and the Sailing Crew of Maiden Made Nautical History," *The New Yorker*, July 22, 2019). Edwards points out that Fisher "allowed his mind to change." In an interview with Fisher, Edwards said, "Bob, you have come a long way! And he said, 'Well, I had a good teacher'" (in "Tracy Edwards Still Breaking the Waves," *The Ex-Press*, July 24, 2019).

[8] Schulman, "How Tracy Edwards and the Sailing Crew of Maiden Made Nautical History."

[9] Mary Alice Miller, "Open Sea: The Remarkable True Story of *Maiden*," *Vanity Fair*, June 27, 2019.

participated in a refurbished *Maiden*'s round-the-world excursion, a promotion to raise funds for the education of girls.[10]

The most spectacular scene of the film is the *Maiden*'s return to Southampton, the port it had left nine months before. The crew feels terrible that they haven't won the race; they face a future that is bleakly anticlimactic after the drama of the high seas. Then, gradually, one by one, without a word, small boats appear, until a whole armada surrounds them. As a gentleman on a rival sailboat comments, "They weren't here to see us; they were here to welcome *Maiden*." Indeed, that convoy of little boats escorting the one that's been around the world could be the visual to accompany many women's less newsworthy lives.

Like Mary and Salome, they spend a lifetime doing the next task, moving one step at a time ahead with no idea of a larger picture. Then, if they are lucky, they see how launching one student, one documentary, one family, one court case, one small business, one piece of legislation, one school, one art or music or medical or social justice project is part of the bigger whole. No one sees the hidden companions, but soul-sisters accompany, like quiet boats in the Southampton harbor: Saint Claire, Saint Brigid, the four women doctors of the church, Saint Jane de Chantal, Saint Mary MacKillop. "Ah, so we weren't alone. We were accompanied all that time. No matter how minor our contribution seemed, we made a difference." Cue the quiet symphony.

As for the failure of men's closed ranks to discuss the women's experience and testimony, "today that conversation remains the 'unfinished business' of the resurrection, an inclusion of women's testimony yet to be realized in the Church of Peter."[11]

Finding the Sweet Spices: Salome Remembers

When the sabbath was over, Mary Magdalene, and Mary the mother of James, and Salome bought spices, so that they

[10] Alex Andrejev, "Her Mom Broke Barriers with an All-Female Crew," *Washington Post*, July 4, 2019.

[11] Rosenblatt, "Women in the Passion and Resurrection Narratives," 51.

might go and anoint him. And very early on the first day of the week, when the sun had risen, they went to the tomb. (Mk 16:1–2)

I found the jar in the
shadows of a shelf,
years later. Inching
open the dusty lid, fragrance
brought it all back: the fear-filled
morning, milky before
dawn, exhausted friends'
faces, red-eyed with
crying and no sleep.
"Let's do what we can"
our inglorious resolve.

I'm still embarrassed
that we ran terrified from
one who told us not to fear.
Were we fleeing something
in ourselves, that I know now
resurrects? Was the news
too good to believe?
I swirl these tiny spice grains
like puzzle pieces, wondering:
the fact we never used them,
their scent now slightly stale,
does it prove something stupendous?

QUESTIONS FOR REFLECTION AND DISCUSSION

1. Have you experienced the futility of watching injustice from a distance, unable to intervene? Does it give you some insight into how the women of Galilee felt at Jesus's crucifixion? How did Jesus share their same passivity, unable to change events?

2. What about waiting at a tomb? Anything comparable in your experience? How did you contend with that?

3. What examples would you add to those of Nadine Burke Harris and Tracy Edwards of women's surprising resilience and dramatic achievement, sometimes in the face of difficult odds?

PART II

WOMEN IN METAPHOR AND PARABLE

16

The Bakerwoman

(LUKE 13:20–21; MATTHEW 13:33)

Baking was an art that I'd learned from my grandmother and had once hoped to pass on to my daughter. I reveled in sprinkling leaven across a lump of dough, then working it with strong fingers like a potter with clay. The yeasty smell would fill the house, and I'd watch that graceful arc rise beneath the towel with the same fascination as the children did. We were easily entertained!

One child, my sister Miriam's boy, Jesus, seemed especially intrigued. He'd line up with the rest of them, a scruffy bunch awaiting their hot slice as soon as the bread came out of the oven. Their grimy, hopeful faces reminded me of Psalm 81, where God says: "Open your mouth wide, and I will fill it" (Ps 81:10). At the time, I didn't pay much attention to Jesus, too preoccupied with where I'd get the flour for the next loaf.

My efforts then to keep a family fed seemed so small. How would I ever guess they'd grow—gradually and invisibly as yeast—into something big? My sister was always so proud of her son, and I'll admit he was an unusual young man. So I listened carefully one day as she described his teaching. We were in the kitchen together; I was kneading as usual. My nephew didn't teach in the synagogues, but in the open streets, marketplaces, and homes—maybe so women could hear him. (Quietly, we cherished that innovation. To publicize it might enrage the religious leaders even more.) Anyway, Miriam said he compared the kingdom of heaven to the yeast used by a woman like myself.

That worried me at first. It would get him in trouble, since in scripture leaven meant corruption or evil. My ancestors, fleeing Egypt, had no time for the dough to rise. Their fast escape makes my process seem slow and leisurely now, a regular, rhythmic part of each day. But mixing up the symbols, reversing ideas of who is holy, presenting someone like myself, surely impure in the holiness codes, as a God figure? *That* would arouse the anger of the authorities. Lying awake and restless at night, I'd worry about him as I might about a daughter.

But the more I thought about it, I liked the idea of grace working slowly, imperceptibly, lifting us in ways we couldn't see. I liked the *sureness* of it, since something must be terribly wrong for the yeast not to rise. That suggested a God we could count on, a forgiveness that never balked at our stupidity but just kept flowing. This wasn't a God hemmed in by the hundreds of laws the rabbis cooked up. And what kind of God is this, who doesn't shower us with gold coins (not that we'd mind), but instead gives us nuggets of food? This God seems to care more about daily nurture than extravagant display. The rabbis handed down laws, but God gave manna; Jesus would give bread.

It took me back to that frightening time before he was born. Yes, I was there at the beginning. Miriam had confided in me the news of her unexpected pregnancy, maybe hoping I could stay calmer than our parents would. My heart ached for her, sweet younger sister who was never deliberately unkind. I had no idea how to resolve her dilemma, but I agonized with her.

Then she told me of the terrible tenderness of Joseph. He knew the unbendable penalty for a girl in her predicament. He was also frightened he would lose her, when he'd looked forward to spending the rest of his life with her. It seemed like an impossible choice: he wanted to remain faithful to his tradition but avoid the cruel laws of the tribe. Joseph found a third way, which would still cost him dearly: divorcing her quietly (Mt 1:19).

Neither Miriam nor I ever guessed what made him take her into his home as his wife. Maybe we were too relieved to ask. But those two together trusted God so completely, their son must have absorbed it as naturally as breathing. They must have taught him, too, that God's mercy was larger than any book of law or sacred text. Their conviction gave those three a confident reliance, a leaning-on-God-no-matter-what, that I envied.

When I knew Miriam was going to celebrate Passover with her son and his friends, I insisted on baking. It was the one thing I did well, and I wanted to send my best loaf—the unique gift only I could give—with her that evening. Telling me about it later, she smiled wryly. The disciples, instead of recognizing the importance of this last meal, and behaving in a calm, noble way, bickered about who was most important. (Guess they hadn't really grown up, those boys who once had waited for hot bread in my kitchen!)

Later, I heard rumors that haven't been confirmed, but that I'd like to believe. He broke *my* bread, blessed it, and gave it to them saying, "Take and eat; this is my body." Now, I don't begin to understand what that means, but I suspect that, from the quiet corners of my kitchen, came something so magnificent that it would fill and feed the world. I find myself repeating his lovely words to the rhythm of the kneading. Maybe I never had a daughter, but what a nephew!

The Bakerwoman Today

Most women now want more than domestic baking for a career, with the notable exception of cupcake shops and exotic bakeries springing up everywhere! In ancient times, one scholar estimates, women would spend almost two hours a day "growing grains, soaking and grinding them, mixing, rising and baking them."[1] Today, few have that much time to spend baking, but the bakerwoman captures a universal desire: she delights in her art and how it feeds others.

Whether women are running hospitals or designing software, they still find joy in creative outlets, and as a bonus, sharing their talents with others. Tell them their work is holy, and they stiffen in protest. Maybe it's easier to convince them that Jesus works with our smallest efforts and skills to bring the world another quarter-inch in line with his dream for what creation could be.

Some women seem to know instinctively that the best cure for a cranky adolescent or brooding grandma is to pull out the pan for cinnamon rolls. Others know that there's no cure for grief, but they'll do what they can, and bring zucchini bread. People are naturally drawn to their kitchens to relish the taste, the fragrance, the texture, the artistry. Like the boy, Jesus, imagined here, we're all hungry kids at heart. The adult Jesus might have remembered his aunt when he fed the five thousand with fish and *barley loaves.* For those accustomed to shrinking quantities, he even provided leftovers, surety for the next day! (Jn 6:5–13).

Bread played an important part in Jesus's life: at the beginning, when he was laid in a feeding trough for animals, and Bet Lehem means "House of Bread"; in the middle where we read of the miracles of feeding; and at the end, when he shared bread with his friends, told them it was his body, and asked them to remember him in it. Throughout Jesus's life, then, bread was a touchstone; bread enclosed him like brackets. How significant, too, that he chose as a way to remember him something eaten by most of the world's peoples in one form or another, a staple of most diets everywhere.

The last supper contrasts dramatically with the feast given by Herod in Matthew 14:1–12. The wine there is excellent, the bread plentiful, the meat the finest, and the guests the upper crust. But Herodias's daughter demands a different dish, and the head of

---

[1] Carol Newsome and Sharon Ringe, eds., *The Women's Bible Commentary* (Louisville, KY: Westminster/John Knox Press, 1992), 247.

John the Baptist is served her on a platter.[2] Ironically, the simpler, final meal represented genuine nurture. By the same token, people in five-star restaurants are sometimes so distracted by their phones or their arguments that they're not even tasting the gourmet food they eat. And a small family at the end of the day can relish its mac 'n' cheese and "how was your day?" conversation.

Mother Teresa of Calcutta wrote of Jesus coming to us as the hungry one.[3] It's an interesting reversal, because we so often think of *him* as feeding *us*. But the idea may remind us of all the meals we've made for hungry people in homes and soup kitchens, church dining halls and restaurants, rarely recognizing his hunger in ordinary faces. The snack we make for the small child is offered as a desperate plea for quiet, but does the hand of Christ reach out for it?

When Jesus said, "I am the bread of life" (Jn 6:48), he touches a deep chord with human beings. Feeding hunger is a far more common, everyday experience than reading books, admiring art, studying law, playing music, worshiping, or discussing philosophy. He reminds us of the most wonderful meals we've had with loved ones, living or dead now. He evokes the earliest memories of home, which may continue into the present. To all who cherish tables encircled by family or friends, he says, "This is who I am." One scholar describes him as "one of ourselves—fond of his food and drink! Whatever else their significance, the meals Jesus took in company reveal his simple acceptance of the smiling side of life."[4]

He gives us nurturing experiences in this life to prepare us for the eternal table, where no one squabbles, stresses, is excluded, or worries how to pay for the meal. The tables where we've eaten happily form steppingstones to the perfect banquet, where the

---

[2] Rose Marie Berger, "The Miracle of Christmas Bread," in *Goodness and Light: Readings for Advent and Christmas* (Maryknoll, NY: Orbis Books, 2015), 165. See also Chapter 3 above.

[3] In *Give Us This Day*, Liturgical Press, May 7, 2015.

[4] Ruth Burrows, *Essence of Prayer* (Mahwah, NJ: Paulist/Hiddenspring, 2006), 104.

milk won't sour or the dish become empty. For most people the metaphor of bread, expanded into table and home, is richly evocative. It gives us a concrete, joyful, accessible entry into what God has prepared for a life in which time and space no longer constrain.

QUESTIONS FOR REFLECTION AND DISCUSSION

1. The bakerwoman stands in a long lineage: the three measures of flour she uses was approximately the same amount used by Sarah baking for "visitors," angels who predicted her pregnancy (Gen 18:6), and Hannah, who offers the flour to Eli in the house of the Lord, along with her young child Samuel (1 Sam 1:24).

So, too, we would not be the women we are without those who came before us. Without taking the baking metaphor too literally, what women do you look to as foremothers (not biologically, but for their nurturing)? We know how capably women ran abbeys during the Middle Ages or later, began religious orders to care for the poor, sick, and uneducated when governments didn't assume those roles. For centuries they have parented, sung, nursed, taught, sculpted, cooked, driven, sewn, researched, woven, cured, guided, argued, painted, led, built, composed, legislated, coaxed, organized, written, danced, planted, cleansed, brought beauty, and made countless contributions to our world. Think of one woman who has brought you delight or guidance. Picture her in your imagination. Savor her gifts. Think how flat life might be without her. Then, if she is alive, write, phone, email, or text your thanks. If she is no longer alive, thank someone else who is.

2. Even those who don't bake bread know the principle of leavening. From tiny grains grows something large and delicious. The same principle could apply to the small embryo becoming a six-foot son, dark seeds in a garden becoming cornstalks, or the slight kernel of an idea becoming a major project in reality.

Looking at your own life, where do you see something that began small growing into something surprisingly big? How do you think Jesus came to understand that principle? Where else does he use it in his teaching?

3. We've all seen countless works of art depicting the last supper. But few include portraits of those behind the scenes who cooked it and cleaned it up afterward. Most surely they were women. What others can you imagine, besides the bakerwoman, who contributed to the meal? What were their stories before and after that threshold event? In what ways might it have changed them?

4. The previous question leads to a larger one: who were the homemakers and financial supports in Jesus's life, besides Mary his mother? (see Lk 8:1–3.) He must have had some good experiences with them, to say so beautifully, "Abide in me as I abide in you" (Jn 15:4).

5. What meals were highlights in your life? Where were they? Who was there? What did you eat or drink? After listing some, think of them all rolled into one, with the people who are dead now being present there, any flaws erased, the happiness magnified endlessly. Reflect further that everyone has access, payment is unnecessary, everything is freely given, and no worrisome calories accumulate around the hips. No one anywhere in the world hungers any longer. That image is a foretaste of heaven!

17

The Woman Who Lost the Coin

(Luke 15:8–10, 21:1–4; Mark 12:41–44)

I couldn't manage money, but I excelled at parties. My story has three markers.

Part 1

It began when I was a young mother. I remember Jesus watching that day as I burrowed through the muck on the floor, desperate to find that coin. Of all my son's friends, he was the most thoughtful, slightly more serious than the other boys. They were all so young then, absorbed in play. Most of them barely noticed my dilemma. But Jesus was different. It was as if he stored my experience in some quiet trove that he'd bring forth years later.

But as I said, I wasn't paying much attention to him. I needed that coin badly, and my only form of safekeeping had failed. Back then, we were desperately poor, and that coin meant meals for the family. I berated myself as I hunted and swept: how could I be so careless?

When I finally heard the clink against the broom, I let out a hoot that the children could hear outdoors. That silver gleamed from a dusty corner like a fallen star. I grasped it tightly in my fist as I danced around our little home, exuberant. But what's good news without girlfriends? *This* was the time to celebrate. Word spreads quickly through my neighborhood, and soon we collected a few treats the children rarely have, a little wine for the adults, and presto! A party.

Jesus was part of it all, solemnly chewing his sweet with the other children. I gave it little thought afterward. But whenever times were tight or money scarce, I returned to that joy. It continued to fill me, brimming over with the coppery glow of an inner treasure.

PART 2

Twenty years later I'd learned I couldn't control everything. That found coin I had clenched so close was quickly spent, as were others that followed. Maybe as I aged I relaxed with money as with everything else. I learned I had no say about what's most important. Much as I pleaded with God to save my husband's life, he died anyway. Sunk in sorrow, I agreed when a friend wanted me to hear the new preacher in town. She'd been so kind through my grief and depression, it seemed like a small inconvenience to accompany her that day.

Oddly enough, this rabbi didn't speak in the synagogue. The gossips said he didn't do well there. And I couldn't have gone anyway. Our town is poor and can't afford a second story for the women. Since we *must* worship separately (why would our praying together offend God?), only the men went to services. I was glad I could hear this rabbi teach outdoors, in the open air, without all the stifling male ritual.

You can imagine my astonishment when he spoke of something so familiar, so close to home that it seemed to rise up from within me. "Or what woman having ten coins and losing one . . . " Suddenly, I was young again, desperately lighting a lamp and peering into the dusty corners.

I pushed forward to look more closely at the speaker. How could he have known my story? Then I heard his name. Jesus had been there for the loss and the finding, the party that followed. From my frustration he carved a parable. Maybe it's true that we find God when we fail. I was at my worst that day, but he made me a figure of God.

PART 3

So the joy continued afterward. I always remembered how *my* lost coin showed God seeking out the lost ones. If God was as persistent as I had been, how could I not feel secure? Not only was the coin found: *I* was too! It was almost as if I knew God from within, as closely as one of my friends. A few women had gone through it all with me: the marriages and births, the tragedies and celebrations, the illnesses and deaths. Imagine that: God as close as one of these companions! The rabbis had never told me that. But I knew the only way it counts—firsthand.

Parties were rare in our village, and maybe we enjoyed them more because they didn't come often. But after I heard Jesus's parable, I understood; the party is within me. The gratitude spilled over again, as it had so many years ago.

Feeling blessed, I took two coins to the temple. I returned one for the coin that had long ago been lost and found. I brought the other for the sheer, free giving of it. A deep river of happiness swept aside worry and greed—no room for them there. Despite poverty, my life had been graced: dear parents, faithful friends, a loving husband, and healthy children. Then, too, the daily blessings: the candlelight falling on the sabbath dinner; the smell of rain on the dust; the invigorating cool of morning as I kindled the cooking fire; and the honeyed taste of challah bread. What more could anyone ask?

Dayenu is one of our oldest prayers, and I said it to myself as I walked to the temple.

If God had only rescued us from Egypt,
but not opened the sea for us—
it would have been enough.

If God had only opened the sea for us,
but not supplied us with manna in the desert—
it would have been enough.

If God had only supplied us with manna in the desert,
but not made a covenant with us—
it would have been enough.

I always added my own variations:

If God had given me only one friend,
but not given me many—
it would have been enough.

If God had given me only many friends,
but not a fine husband as well—
it would have been enough.

If God had given me only a fine husband,
but not many children—
it would have been enough.

Money seemed secondary to such blessing. The coins clinking into the treasury had a familiar, metallic ring. Then I remembered: a found coin had sounded like that once. The coins weren't worth much, but giving of myself—that, as always, was pure gold. When I dropped them in, they chimed like bells. Even some bystanders noticed.

The Woman Who Lost the Coin Today

It's admittedly a stretch of the imagination to suggest that the woman who lost the coin in the parable of Luke 15 might be the same widow whom Jesus praised for giving her last two coins to the temple treasury. But if we use Midrash imaginatively to fill in the long arc of her life, the two events seem compatible enough that they might have been the actions of the same person.

While that is speculation, the larger, stunning reality is that Jesus presents a woman as a figure of God. Remember the low status of women in his day. Scripture scholar Barbara Reid develops more fully what Jesus suggests in story. Because the woman is entrusted with household finances and management, "the woman seeking the coin is a metaphor equally apt for speaking of God as is 'father.'" A woman who "expends every effort for the sake of the lost" exemplifies Jesus, pouring out life for others. "These stories challenge us to see that in women, as well as men, Christ is fully embodied."[1]

One reading of the Mark story, the woman who gives her last two coins, is a condemnation of the scribes who bilk the poor. By extension, it's a warning to women who think they're doing a godly thing by pouring out life in service so completely that they have no life of their own, or have no true center from which to give of themselves. Some women need boundaries; some need to learn to say no; and others must ask for what they genuinely need.

The story suggests many years' experience between the two events. During that time, of ordinary days and festivals, loving and being loved, ups and downs, the woman could have developed a mature freedom that lacks nothing. She could have grown from one who grasps the lost coin to one who lets it slide easily through her fingers. How could coins compare with the unending wealth of grateful memory? "If the widow's gift of self is given with free choice out of love, then she *is* the feminine counterpart of Jesus."[2]

---

[1] Barbara Reid, *Women in the Gospel of Luke* (Collegeville, MN: Liturgical Press, 1996), 188, 207.

[2] Barbara Reid, *Taking Up the Cross* (Minneapolis: Augsburg Fortress, 2007), 49–50.

QUESTIONS FOR REFLECTION AND DISCUSSION

1. If you were to place Luke's parable of the lost coin in a contemporary setting, what might the woman lose? Her iPhone? Her glasses? Her keys? What is as valuable to you as the coin must have been to her? How would you feel upon finding it?

2. In this parable Jesus asks us to reflect on our experience, as he so often does. Over the years, as you have defined and redefined your role, have you lost anything along the way?

- Some excess baggage, that no longer serves you?
- Something that you once cherished?
- What have you found?

3. When the narrator finds the coin, it's a second chance. Jesus doesn't blame her for the loss or hound her for being irresponsible. Jesus delights in the celebration! When have you gotten a second chance (or twentieth or two thousandth)? Here, you could include the car accident averted, the relationship restored, the job loss that led to a greater gain, the healing after illness, the familiar, old home exchanged for an even better one, and so on.

4. Jesus's resurrection, shared with us is the ultimate second chance—eternal life after a limited life on earth—and it never ends! What memories or experiences have become to you more valuable than money?

5. Write or pray your own version of the narrator's *Dayenu*. Here's the form:

If God had given me only_____________,
but not_____________—
it would have been enough.

Repeat as often as you wish, filling in the blanks.

18

The Foolish Bridesmaid

(MATTHEW 25:1–13)

For centuries I've been called foolish. But you haven't heard my side of the story.

When my cousin Esther invited me to be part of her wedding party, I twirled with excitement. It was as if she had offered me the key to another country. I explored this world with the fascination of discovering a new continent for the first time.

It was hard to understand marriage, because my parents detested each other. Often the last noise I heard before falling asleep was my father beating my mother and her frightened, muffled cry. Her bruises in the morning were pitiful, but even worse was her attempt to hide them and protect him. When I caught the scent of something different in *this* wedding, I paid attention.

Esther's groom, Mical, wasn't handsome; in fact, he was pudgy. But he treated her like his dearest friend. When he wanted another opinion, he didn't just ask his male buddies; *her* voice mattered. They laughed together often; they walked with the same rhythm. He touched her with tenderness, and she shimmered. His voice was gentle; I couldn't imagine him yelling like my father, constantly berating my mother. Cool soup or moldy bread threw dad into a tirade that made me flee the house. But Mical was kind, even to me, the snotty-nosed young cousin with the bad haircut.

I guess I was secretly in love with him—all the bridesmaids were. In his company we all felt beautiful and cherished, because we were important to Esther.

Since I'd never been in a wedding, I didn't know about bringing extra oil. We'd all dozed off that night, when Mical was detained. The first thing I knew was my sister poking me, demanding my lamp. Half awake, I gave it to her grudgingly. They say when I was small, I'd toddle around behind her, repeating everything she said. I adored my big sister. I tried to imitate her actions, and surely she knew this wedding business better than I did. So I was puzzled when she told me to go buy more oil. Was this job foisted on the youngest? And where could I buy oil at midnight?

Into my confusion, as I sleepily searched for oil, gradually seeped one painful truth. I'd be locked out of the banquet. For months I'd fantasized about that feast. I would imagine *that* world whenever my parents nipped at each other or the food on our table was scarce. I would wear a special gown, gossamer and silvery, swishing around my ankles. I would eat the choicest meal. I might even dance with the groom. All my favorite foods, and some I'd only smelled on the breeze, drifted through my imagination. Guess I was so hungry for everything that wedding represented that losing it felt like a blow to the stomach.

Trudging through darkness to find oil, I discovered my sister had concocted a fake errand to get rid of me and use my lamp. The patterns of lamplight played beautifully on trees and walls, but I could watch only from a distance. Exhausted with disbelief and disappointment, I wept outside the hall. I could hear the distant music; I could picture Mical looking deep with care into Esther's eyes. The wine I'd longed to taste gleamed forever out of reach. Bent double, I sobbed into my beautiful dress and ruined its sheen. No one rescued me; there was no magic ending to the story.

It reminded me of the story that the prophet Nathan told David about a rich man. Reluctant to take one of his many flocks and herds to feed a traveler, he instead took the only lamb of a poor man, who had nurtured this ewe "like a daughter." David was outraged by that arrogance and said the rich man deserved to die. "'Ah,' said Nathan, 'That man is you'" (2 Sam 12:1–10).

I thought of the story because I too had cherished one dream. I didn't have much; I wanted so badly to be in that wedding. Nathan was subtly pointing to another marriage: David expeditiously having Uriah killed so he could marry Bathsheba, the widow. David admitted his guilt, and his first son died as a consequence. But I was troubled; my sister had stolen everything I yearned for. Still, I didn't want her to die for her lie. I told myself repeatedly, "You'll get over it." But still, it grated, making my loneliness worse. Every night as I fell asleep, I thought of that door shutting, or I dreamed of the lamplight on the leaves.

Several years later, though, the old sadness was somewhat resolved. I heard a man named Jesus tell my story, but he'd given it a new twist. "The kingdom of heaven," whatever that meant, would be like the feast I'd missed. That snagged my attention. Would I get a second chance? Could I finally sail, erect and gracious, through that door that once was locked? But the next part made the hair on the back of my neck prickle. God, in the story, was like Mical. That call I'd heard in my sleep could come again: "Behold the bridegroom! Come out to meet him!"

He seemed to be saying that God, like Mical, was gentle, brimming with life and joy, energized by Esther's presence. Could God still look tenderly on me, who had failed so miserably to serve as a wise bridesmaid? I'm intrigued by the possibility, or maybe I'm just desperate. For years I'd been taught that God was like my father, so I wanted to escape. But *this* new comparison gleams with possibility! No more sleeping on the job; this is a God I want to run and meet. *This* God is bride and groom, wine and feast, lamp and friend, wedding and joy.

Next time, I'll be ready.

FOOLISH BRIDESMAID TODAY

The Jews of Jesus's day believed that a wedding was the sign of God's reign. People were exempt from some religious duties to participate. Many people still believe that Christ comes again and again—in joy, not as a dire threat. The question the parable raises is one of preparation. Do we look for divine surprises in every day, no matter how routine it is? Can we delight in the unexpected phone call or text, the contours of ripe peach, the abundance of the grocery store, the skill of the dentist or doctor, the secure predictability of sunrise and sunset, the sheen of red maple leaves, the opening of an email as if roses would spill from the computer?

For centuries the foolish bridesmaids have gotten a bum rap. But could there be another side to the story? How could it continue, after the wedding ends and the party is cleaned away? Surely God would give a second chance to someone who acted out of ignorance. Hasn't *everyone* been unprepared for *something*, no matter how important?

QUESTIONS FOR REFLECTION AND DISCUSSION

1. How did you respond to the foolish bridesmaid portrayed in a more sympathetic light? Did it disrupt familiar ways of thinking and perhaps open new possibilities on other Bible stories too?
2. Imagine a second chance for the bridesmaid who narrates this story.
3. Have you ever gotten a second chance? If so, describe it. If not, what do you still long for God to give?
4. For people with abusive fathers, the idea of God as father is problematic. Domestic abuse and violence are still rampant. Even in "enlightened" countries, many women must struggle with that paternal image of God. What other images might be more helpful to them?
5. The mystic Julian of Norwich says that God is a lover who finds in humanity bliss and delight. Does that idea accord with or change your image of God? How?

19

The Persistent Widow

(LUKE 18:1–8)

Sometimes during the night, half awake, I still reach for his hand. Then comes the moment of horrid realization: he's not there. I usually lie awake for a long time after that, but I find the best remedy for sleeplessness is to review memories of our marriage. I start with the first time I saw him. He was skinny, handsome, and painfully young. So was I. But something kindled between us that still hasn't been extinguished thirty years later, even after his death.

Oh, we weren't perfect. We betrayed each other and argued and sulked and hurt each other with a cruelty I'd never thought possible at the beginning. How do people who once spoke sweetly start criticizing and demeaning each other?

Maybe life eroded that first harmony with worries about money, food and shelter, illnesses, and squabbles over childrearing. Sometimes we couldn't bear the painful conversations, so we'd skirt the issues. I'd sometimes ask my sisters' advice, but they and their husbands were mired in the same swamp. All of us struggled to survive, went to sleep exhausted and woke too early, still tired.

It wasn't always tough. We also had joyful stretches, times of gratitude and learning, feeling awake and alive. We'd hear a song we both liked or a good story that made us laugh. He'd rub my neck at the end of the day when my shoulders felt like stone. A holiday would restore our best selves, rested at last after dancing at a festival and eating well. Always, there was the great peace of returning to each other's warmth at night. Our marriage, like most I guess, contained lonely pockets of irritation and deep bowls of blessing.

Despite all his other flaws, my husband was a hard worker, protective of our family, looking out for our future. I worked hard beside him, helping our family survive. Gradually, he built our home and enlarged our tiny plot of land. He sweated over every beam raised for the roof, every crop planted in our garden. Even when he got sick, he wanted to preserve what he'd worked so hard to provide. He knew the misery that awaited widows in our society. Without a son, I'd definitely be poor and possibly homeless. He did everything he could to protect me from disaster.

Toward the end of his illness, some said he looked gaunt. I saw only the slender face of that boy I'd loved long ago. He couldn't speak, but the yearning in his eyes said, "Everything is forgiven, forgotten." I recounted our finest memories as I sat beside his deathbed, thinking as I told the stories: "At least this is one thing I can do. Maybe I can help him remember the best times, so he can die with some happiness. And after death, we'll love better than we did in life."

Later, when he'd fallen into a deep sleep, I lay beside him, and suddenly the air in the room shifted. He was no longer breathing, but the hand I reached for was still warm. "You were always a helper," I whispered to him. "Keep doing it now with dazzling power. I haven't been alone in thirty years and have no idea how to do it now!" I doubled over in raw pain, thinking that the world seemed a less protected place since he'd left behind a gaping hole.

I'd often wondered about a verse from Isaiah: "The Lord God will wipe away the tears from all faces" (Isa 25:8). How could God possibly do that? All around me faces were covered with tears. My eyes were red for months. God must have a handkerchief the size of the universe! But step by step, I saw how it could happen.

While I was still in shock, my neighbor offered to help. In the blur of grief his offer sounded generous. He'd "look after things" until I got on my feet. My daughters lived far away; I had no brother. Since few hands were offered in help, I desperately grabbed the one that seemed lifesaving. Stupid and weak, I agreed to his plan. Little did I know that this was his slimy way of encroaching on what was rightly mine.

By the time I realized clearly what had happened, that snake had all the right words to defend his theft: "I was only looking out for your good. Of course, you understand why, after so much time, it's mine now." He'd cunningly seized the land we worked so hard to get? That turf my husband wanted me to have, my only inheritance? I filled with a rage I'd never before felt, as if a fist lodged in my throat. During many sleepless nights I searched for ways to defend myself. I'd always been quiet and polite. How would I ever confront that huge, corrupt system of justice in our town?

One condescending comment from the neighbor finally drove me to the judge: "No court in the land would pay attention to you, little woman." Of course, he was right. Women counted for less than oxen in my world, but I had to try. If I didn't, I'd fail my husband. But even more important, I'd fail myself. After all those years of leaning on my husband, I had to stand up for myself. I was on my own now—if I didn't look out for me, who would? Maybe God was on my side too—a formidable force!

The anger burned bright enough to fuel my search for justice. No matter how often that judge "patted me on the head" and told me to get lost, I would return. I had no weapon but stubbornness and the conviction that my cause was just. The judge dismissed me more times than I can count and repeatedly told me he was "acting on my behalf"—what would *I* know about managing land?

"Precious little," I'd have said if I answered truthfully. But I wouldn't give him even the slightest doubt, a chink in my armor. I smile when I recall how gradually I wore him down. It even surprises me to see how annoying I became, I who was once well behaved. There were days when I'd tire of the trek to see the judge again. But then I'd think, "What am I doing that's more important?" Or I'd see our land in an afternoon slant of light, radiant with new green shoots, or I'd remember my husband's pride as he bought one tiny parcel after another, hoping he'd enrich my old age.

Then I'd roar like a mother bear protecting her cubs, and set off again. Each time that judge saw me coming, he probably groaned and sent out the gatekeepers to protect himself. But even they came around to my side, maybe remembering a mother or sister who'd also been abandoned. They'd smuggle me in, and it was a hoot to see his face crumple at the sight of me—again.

I don't know what persuaded him, but one day he capitulated. Maybe he feared I'd grow violent. Maybe he was just exhausted. Maybe he saw an easier way to line his slick pocket. But it didn't matter why or how. Sometimes, I think, God must use human hands to wipe away the tears on our faces. Surely God and I were in cahoots as I pursued my cause. That quest helped me work through my grief, so now and then I feel a surprising tickle of joy.

I must admit that I'm proud, too. That once frightened girl had gained a steel spine, a conviction about justice, and a strong voice that at first was almost unrecognizable. It could even be that the judge did me a favor. Every time I'd see his stony face, his locked jaw, I'd stand taller, grow stronger. Now I even stick up for my friends when they're victims. I've learned to walk alone. Within me had hidden some formidable forces. With great satisfaction I sit on my porch, admire our land, remember my husband, and whisper, "I've kept it, dear."

The Persistent Widow Today

This parable could be titled "How Women Can Be a Pain in the Neck" or "The Annoying Female Disrupts the Orderly Legal System" or "Her Shrieks Rattle the Way It's Always Been." This version presents the widow with more sympathy than she's usually regarded. It stands squarely within the *mashal* tradition—the use of short parables to teach moral lessons. Cynthia Bourgeault points out that "Jesus not only taught within this tradition, he turned it end for end."[1]

His interest was in the intimate human happening, the daily routines that some have named the scandal of the ordinary. His stories focus far more on individuals and families than on the vast questions of international politics, Roman oppression, the relationship of church and state, or the role of a messiah—issues he continually avoided. Instead, he spoke about a small field—probably, in our world, the size of a postage stamp—the tug of war over ownership, the conniving greed of one who'd cheat a widow, her stalwart resistance. Bourgeault continues:

> He stayed close to the ground of wisdom: the transformation of human consciousness. He asked timeless and deeply personal questions: What does it mean to die before you die? How do you go about losing your little life to find the bigger one? Is it possible to live on this planet with a generosity, abundance, fearlessness, and beauty that mirror Divine Being itself?
>
> These are the wisdom questions, and they are the entire field of Jesus's concern.[2]

Jesus asks whether God would not be *better* than the judge: not slow to answer, but quickly doing justice. It's hard to believe when we're in a tough situation, but sometimes God sends the difficult person or experience to teach something we need to learn. In the long run the judge who seemed a cruel opponent might have done the widow a huge favor. His resistance helped her come into her own sense of voice and conviction of justice. She emerges

---

[1] Cynthia Bourgeault, *The Wisdom Jesus: Transforming Heart and Mind: A New Perspective on Christ and His Message* (Boulder, CO: Shambhala, 2008), 23–24.

[2] Bourgeault, 23–24.

eventually as a formidable force—and comes to peace within. Some scholars believe the parables are like koans in the Zen tradition—nudges from our established ways of thinking, our easy divisions between good and bad, right and wrong, in and out.[3]

The stories remind us painfully how coolly expedient we can be to get rid of something that stands in the way of what we want. How quickly we dismiss another's idea or opinion if it doesn't align completely with our own. How we ridicule some cherished possession that might appear to us like a cheap trinket, but for the owner holds invaluable memories or a family heritage. Jesus cut close to the bone with this story, knowing how dark our hidden urges can sometimes be. He didn't shy away from the uglier, greedier side of human nature and drift somewhere aloft, where only fragrant lilies bloom. Where is God in the mess of stealing from a widow and exploiting the vulnerable?

Some may be puzzled by this entry into the "darker side," but others turn the tables: seeing the Godlike figure as the woman, not the judge. William Bausch asks, "Is the message that if you badger God long enough you can eventually wear God down and get what you want?" Problematic! Instead, he sees the woman "as powerless as Jesus on the cross," but through her fidelity becoming a "kind of Gandhi or Martin Luther King figure. Against all odds she will endure until justice is done."[4]

Jesus's immersion into this darker arena is echoed in the finding of a small but lovely Marian statue among brambles and thorns. The Sanctuary of Our Lady of Arantzazu, in Spain, founded by the Franciscans in 1501, shelters that unlikely presence. According to legend, Mary appeared to a shepherd in 1468; he cried out, "Arantzan zu?!" (Thou, among the thorns?!) The answer is *yes.* Here too is where Christ stood, embracing the complex tangle of all human experience. This shrine became an important stopping

---

[3] Bourgeault, 50.

[4] William Bausch, *Once upon a Gospel: Inspiring Homilies and Insightful Reflections* (New London/Mystic, CT: Twenty-Third Publications, 2008), 294–95.

point for Saint Ignatius on his journey from the castle of Loyola, trading his sword for a walking stick, going eventually to the Holy Land. He would later write of "finding God in all things," that God who labors mightily to bring even the worst into wholeness.

Questions for Reflection and Discussion

1. Which interpretation do you prefer: God as judge or God as widow? Why?

2. What of the things we cherish? Has anything been as important to you as the land was to the widow? Does that treasure help you understand her better? Does it make you feel vulnerable because it's always at risk, or strengthened to defend it?

3. The narrator goes through a process we might call empowerment, finding her own voice. After years of relying on her husband, she discovers her own inner strengths. Have you, or someone you know, had a similar experience? If so, describe it.

4. When have you persisted in a just cause? Were you satisfied by the result or not?

5. To what extent do you feel unsettled by the parable? Empowered by it? Have you ever learned more from a conflict than from a peaceful agreement? If so, describe that experience.

6. Considering all the arenas of injustice you know personally, where would you most like to speak or hear words of liberation?

7. "Will not God then secure the rights of his chosen ones who call out to him day and night? Will he be slow to answer them? I tell you, he will see to it that justice is done for them speedily" (Lk 18:7–8, NABRE). What's your response to the word *speedily* in this quotation?

PART III

WOMEN IN ACTS

20

Lydia

(Acts 16:14, 40)

I am confident of this, that the one who began a good work among you will bring it to completion by the day of Jesus Christ. (Phil 1:6)

Let the same mind be in you that was in Christ Jesus. (Phil 2:5)

Whatever gains I had, these I have come to regard as loss because of Christ. (Phil 3:7)

Did you ever wonder who Paul had in mind when he wrote these inspiring words? It was I. I'd long been a successful businesswoman, but this was the culmination of my career. I led the house church that first heard the Letter to the Philippians.

But that gets ahead of my story. Some time earlier I'd gone, as usual, to the river outside the city gate with some friends; it was restful there after a hot day. The green shade was peaceful beside the stream after the noise of the marketplace. We were sitting with our feet in cool water, talking quietly, when Paul and Silas arrived. It began as a chance (or graced) encounter and eventually led to Paul describing us as "my brothers and sisters, whom I love and long for, my joy and crown" (Phil 4:1). You must be wondering what happened in between.

My town, Philippi, was a bustling place located on the Greco-Roman trade routes. I was an influential and successful merchant; I sold my finest textiles to wealthy Romans. But being "a dealer in purple cloth" wasn't enough. I thirsted for more. Later the author of Acts would say of me, "The Lord opened her heart to listen eagerly to what was said by Paul" (Acts 16:14).

My questions to Paul opened doors to an inner release. His message spilled into my thirsty spirit like the waters of that stream where we first met. To hear that I was no longer ostracized because of my gender, or class, or religion lifted my spirit and my chin. I wanted to share the best I had, so I had myself and my household (yes, I had that much authority) baptized at once.

After my baptism Paul and Silas were jailed. Later freed by a violent earthquake that loosened their chains, they came straight to my house. Of course, I welcomed them with a radiant party. The Christians gathered to hear the remarkable story, and after the dank prison, the disciples appreciated a fine meal, luxurious tablecloths, and good wine.

My home continued to be a gathering place for Christians. It's easy to picture the word going out on the grapevine: "New letter from Paul!" They would listen eagerly as I read aloud: "Finally, beloved, whatever is true, whatever is honorable, whatever is just, whatever is pure, whatever is pleasing, whatever is commendable, if there is any excellence and if there is anything worthy of praise, think about these things" (Phil 4:8).

LYDIA TODAY

Any skilled writer imagines his or her audience because it affects the theme and choice of words. Writing his famous letter, Paul might have pictured Lydia the first day they met: eyes gleaming, interest kindled, dappled light reflecting off the river onto her purple shawl.

Lydias live all around us; beneath sleek coiffures and designer suits are shrewd minds, hearts eager for truth, and spirits yearning to serve. God's gracious welcome extends to the MBAs and CEOs as warmly as to preschoolers or the poor. It's heartening to know that Jesus speaks not only to the marginalized, for whom he had a special fondness, but appeals as well to the prestigious. The educated and probably affluent magi came to his birthplace as well as the bottom-of-the-social-heap shepherds. He drew not only the diseased and ostracized but also the prosperous.

Lydia and her friends may remind us of many spirituality groups gathered today: coming before work or during lunch hour, dressed in professional clothes, tight on time but eager for meaning and depth. Often they are a mix of Christians, Muslims, and Jews. They study sacred texts of different traditions, or contemporary authors like Rohr, Rupp, Chodron, Heschel, Chittister, Wiederkehr, and Rolheiser. Discussion is lively, and with no time to waste, they cut to the chase. There's little tolerance for pious platitudes; rather, there is a genuine thirst for a more prayerful, compassionate, serene, inclusive way of life.

We can only speculate why a bright, forthright woman like Lydia responded so quickly to Paul. One theory holds that as a woman, possibly a former slave, since the hard work of dyeing was given to them, and a Gentile, she had the "triple whammy" of strikes against her. Her challenging invitation, "If you have judged me to be faithful to the Lord, come and stay at my home" (Acts 16:15), might be Luke's way of saying social inequality had no place in the Christian community. Lydia was independent enough to raise the issue, financially secure with an established business, and "needed nothing from him."[1] If she had transitioned from slave to free, then found the Hebrew God, she might have felt disappointed at Jewish discrimination. So she could have been wary as she put the question, wondering, "Did these Christians practice what they preach?" and delighted at Paul's response.

For Paul to tell her, as he certainly did, that she was God's beloved daughter was transformative. She could have worn the

[1] Florence Gillman, *Women Who Knew Paul* (Collegeville, MN: Liturgical Press, 1992), 37–38.

royal purple with pride since in the Christian world at its best, distinctions between women and men, slaves and free, Gentiles and Jews were totally irrelevant. What mattered was following Christ's way, by innumerable different paths.

Like residents of contemporary cities, the Philippians lived with many distractions. In a trade center it's easy to get caught up in negativity, greed, or competition. Lydia helped the early Christians keep their focus on what mattered. So Paul could say of her and of them all: "In the midst of a crooked and perverse generation . . . you shine like stars" (Phil 2:14).

QUESTIONS FOR REFLECTION AND DISCUSSION

1. Looking around your neighborhood, social circle, or church, where do you find the Lydias today?

2. Lydia has the guts to name controversy and ask Paul the tough question: will you stay at my house, or will you too discriminate against me? What tough questions need to be asked today? Who is asking them, or why are they avoided?

3. If Lydia and Sister Simone Campbell (see Chapter 12) had had a conversation by the river, they might've sparked each other's ideas and nodded in agreement. What other pairings can you imagine between biblical women—real or imagined—and contemporary female leaders? What might they discuss?

4. Create a prayer to Lydia, asking her for the courage to raise the issues that no one else questions in your world.

21

Prisca

(Acts 18:2, 18, 26; Romans 16:3; 1 Corinthians 16:19; 2 Timothy 4:19)

My husband, Aquila, and I were tentmakers. I never dreamt how cutting, sewing, and patching leather would lead to my great work: piecing together the fledgling Christian community like a big tent. Years later, John's prologue would describe the incarnation as God's "pitching a tent in us." Our recorded story began when Paul asked us for a job when he was new in town. He stayed with us for eighteen months in Corinth, where we had already established our business. To set the record straight, Paul didn't convert us; we were already Christian.

It caused some buzz when my name was mentioned before Aquila's (in four of six references), but let me explain. I didn't muscle in to threaten his status; it was simply a natural recognition of my leadership. He was always supportive and strong, but a man of few words. When Apollo came to Ephesus, he spoke boldly and eloquently in the synagogue. But both Aquila and I felt uncomfortable because under all that enthusiasm was a gap in his knowledge. We talked late into the night about how to handle it, and eventually we decided to "take him aside." Of course, it was I who explained more accurately the story we loved, but Aquila's calm presence gave me courage and maybe assured Apollo that he wasn't being criticized by a *woman*—how embarrassing! (Acts 18:26).

I was the talker, better known, but we thought of ourselves as equals, a team. Notice how Paul refers to *our* house, not just Aquila's, as he would if he were to follow more closely the custom of our day. Oh, the male was head of the household in society, but no patriarchy for us! Everyone knew I was the feisty leader.

I wasn't spared the fear of persecution either (Rom 16:3). We risked our necks to save Paul in Ephesus, and after that authorities seemed to know me, to sneer threateningly whenever I'd walk through town. I was so frightened, I persuaded Aquila to return to Rome. Somehow, martyrdom didn't seem the right path for us. Our work was—forgive the pun—cut out for us.

Paul did the original visioning and dramatic speeches. Then he'd turn the new converts over to us. Wise choice. Who knows better than tentmakers how to shelter newborn, vulnerable people? I'd keep them warm and dry. A tent is a flexible place, open to wind and change. Unlike more rigid structures of stone or wood, its flaps can always accommodate one more.

PRISCA TODAY

In her monologue Prisca mentions the fluidity of tents as a metaphor for the Christian community. Indeed, one of the finest metaphors for the church is a big tent. Maybe Prisca spent so much time sticking her neck out to *rescue*, she couldn't be bothered with *excluding*. She might be saddened by the encrustation of rules and exclusions since her day. The original open invitation—"Y'all come!"—has been qualified by a dreary list of "ifs"—*If* you're not divorced and remarried. *If* you believe everything the church teaches. *If* you're not in a committed gay or lesbian relationship. Or even if your *parents* are!

Richard Rohr writes eloquently about the boundary marking, the witch hunts of churches that focus on who *can't* participate. They devote major efforts and energies to judging, condemning, and controlling by shame and guilt. They make God into a petty tyrant rather than the generous host who wants everyone at the banquet. "If there is not room for one more at your party, you are a very poor host. And God is not a poor host."[1]

But rather than simply condemning such behaviors, we can learn from them. James Alison proposes a splendid metaphor of troops advancing. Those who've gotten to higher, safer ground don't waste time making fun of those who are still struggling to get across the battlefield.[2] Instead, they encourage them. So, too, the task for us is not to mock those whose ideas of gender may not be as *obviously* advanced as ours. (Please note the tone of self-deprecation there.) Our task is to get everyone safely to a place where we can all participate fully in the creative, challenging project of being human, without sniping at one another.

What Alison says of the movement for gay and lesbian rights is also true for the women's movement. We are enlarging our notion of being human so that qualifiers such as gender, race, and sexual orientation no longer matter.

Questions for Reflection and Discussion

1. We all like to think of ourselves as inclusive. But is there anyone with whom you wouldn't want to share the close quarters of a tent? Do you reject any part of *yourself* (past actions, words, or attitudes)? Using the metaphor of this chapter, where might Prisca encourage you to open the tent flap wider?

2. Consider the raw courage of women in our own era, participating in the civil rights movement at great personal cost, or marching for farmworkers' rights in *la causa.* How might they in some sense be considered great-great-granddaughters of Prisca, who also risked?

---

[1] Richard Rohr, *Immortal Diamond* (San Francisco: Jossey-Bass, 2013), 110.

[2] Cf. James Alison, *Undergoing God* (New York: Continuum, 2006), 180.

3. Curiously enough, Prisca also does the rather monotonous task of tentmaking. She apparently struck a balance between taking bold risks for the faith and grounding life in daily sewing. How do you find a balance between your homemaking instincts and your desire to strike out for justice? Or have you found one clear and workable path that combines the two?

4. How might Prisca respond to the sight of all male cardinals filing into the Vatican to elect a pope for the Catholic Church, or all male bishops gathering to discuss the family? What might she think of the shift in the US Episcopal Church, in which women clergy outnumber men?

22

Dorcas

(Acts 9:36–42)

It was the sweetest sleep ever. For the first time in ages I didn't need to be busy, achieve or accomplish anything, just rest. I closed my eyes as I'd so often wanted to do, saying in exhaustion, "God, your daughter is tired." No whiny demands, no rude interruptions, no desperate pleas for help could disturb me. Being "completely occupied with good deeds and almsgiving" takes its toll—I was exhausted. But as I slept, I dreamed of the beginning, my first love. I had always loved fabric, the ways that its colors could dance together or light a sallow face. The way it draped across a figure could camouflage the flaws and accent the lovely curves. I've always been intrigued with the contours of cloth, its weight and shimmer in my hands. Into my port city, Joppa, flowed imports from around the world. So I was enchanted with Roman linen, Chinese silk, Arabian sunrises woven into stripes. I imagined women at their looms everywhere, pouring their artistry into this tunic or that skirt.

I too created clothing. My name means "gazelle," and I designed cloaks that swished with the animal's swift grace. Threaded through the garments were the stories: this shirt made for my husband's birthday; that shade matched my daughter's hair or son's eyes.

People who dismiss them as "just clothes" don't get it. Clothes are the vehicle to carry us to an important event or through the demands of an ordinary day. They hold and wrap precious memories in their folds.

When I first heard about Jesus, I was captivated. The man spoke my language—and enlarged it somehow. Of course I was drawn to his examples: "Consider the lilies, how they grow: they neither toil nor spin; yet I tell you, even Solomon in all his glory was not clothed like one of these" (Lk 12:27). I could understand that firsthand. All my spinning and weaving couldn't come near the soft touch of petal or the radiant light of the lily's throat.

Jesus gave me a new focus. Before I heard his message, I'd seen the bodies washed ashore from ships wrecked on the Mediterranean, the many widows and orphans the dead seamen left behind. How pitiful the survivors seemed, wandering the beaches. But gradually, I recognized the one gift I could give them to lessen their pain a little. My sewing could clothe them beautifully; wearing one of my garments, they could walk with a new confidence. As I sewed for them, I tried to capture the lilt of a wave or the deep aqua-blue-gray shadings of the sea outside my window.

But there was so much need, and only one of me, even when my friends helped. Maybe I overdid it, working to exhaustion. One day, I simply couldn't do any more. Smack in the middle of the day, my head pounding and wrists aching, I lay down to rest.

So I was dreaming of a field of wildflowers, bending in the wind. Their color and fragrance filled me with joy. And Jesus was woven in somehow, just as I'd weave a rare gold or copper thread into a fabric. He too knew about not sewing a new patch on an old garment. He understood my world in a way no other teacher did.

As I dozed, I was looking back over my life as though it were a string of laundry hung out to dry. There, in alternating bands of sun and shadow, were some tiny shirts, worn as I learned to walk. One of my favorite Bible passages has always been Hosea:

> When Israel was a child, I loved him,
> and out of Egypt I called my son. . . .

Yet it was I who taught Ephraim to walk,
I took them up in my arms;
but they did not know that I healed them.
I led them with cords of human kindness,
with bands of love.
I was to them like those
who lift infants to their cheeks.
I bent down to them and fed them. (Hos 11:1, 3–4)

In my mind, the passage was illustrated: I knew exactly what color those cords of kindness were and the texture of those bands of love. Stringing my life along a line, I could picture the sleeve tight around the pudgy arm, the bibs for feeding, and the little bonnets mothers so lovingly make for their children as shelter from fierce sun.

Then, the coveted clothes of adolescence—wearing one of those garments was my entry to belonging to a group of friends. I could take my place with pride among the other girls as we strolled through Joppa. Then the detailed embroidery I'd spent days on; every minute was worth it as I twirled with pride at a celebration. The fabric I'd saved for and finally sewed with great joy became my wedding dress, and later, my daughter's.

A sadness shadowed some clothes on the imaginary line. My mother was no longer here to see the garments she'd made me, or my creativity that she'd praised. She was so proud of my skill, and gave me the time and advice to get better. Maybe it was a small stirring of that first primal fear, the worst we can imagine, losing our mother. But when I felt it, I'd burrow into something she'd worn, bury my nose in her familiarity, and find comfort.

Some of my friends were gone, too. We'd compared fabrics and had long, serious discussions about styling. How little we knew, but how important it seemed. The clothes were the vehicle; the friendship remained.

Then a distant growling ended my beautiful rest. Peter, that bear of a man, blundered into my sick room. My cherished friends showed him the tunics I'd embroidered, the cloaks I'd made as strong protection against the heaviest winds. They were wasting their time—the guy didn't know satin from sandwich. But his voice was kind as I heard him say my name as through a tunnel, "Tabitha, rise up." Where had I heard those words before?[1]

The call to life was familiar, but at first I protested. *No*! Let me rest with softly closed eyes. I've earned it. I so enjoyed revisiting the long line of memories. Don't make me everyone's savior again. There's only one, and Jesus is all we need. Enough of do-gooding! Can't I just enjoy that dreamy meadow? But the touch of a hand on mine was warm, comforting, and lifegiving.

As I struggled stiffly to my feet, I remembered others who'd made that precarious journey: the daughter of Jairus, Lazarus, Jesus himself. Death to life was taking on another connotation to me, though. To be God's precious daughter, I didn't need to *do* anything, serve anyone. Since God didn't care about accomplishment, I could take it easier. I could enjoy just being myself. God wasn't nearly the steely-eyed taskmaster I had set up. During that sleepy time of great happiness, I had been still, and free, and blessed. I could do it again. If God so clothed the grass, I too could wear the green gossamer fabric of trust. I rose to a different awareness.

As my vision gradually focuses, I notice that Peter's cloak is ripped. Vaguely, I start planning. I think I'll show him how to thread a needle. . . .

DORCAS TODAY

Not many women today sew or embroider their own clothes as Dorcas did. It was constant, time-consuming work: preparing flax or wool, spinning thread, weaving cloth. Dorcas's role as a seamstress must have meant an investment in time that few could make today. But those hours at a loom or sewing by hand also gave her time to think. She didn't quickly grab a dress off a hanger at a store; she may have made garments to last a lifetime. Seeing

[1] See Lk 8:40–42, 49–56; Mk 5:41: "*Talitha, koum* (maiden, get up)."

the intricate detail of Palestinian or Hmong embroidery today gives us a small glimpse into what the world of clothing might have represented to the women of biblical times.

Even those who haven't made their own clothing know how wearing an item can bring back a whole story: the place we got it, who was with us, if it was a gift from someone we cherish, the elation of a perfect fit or meeting a specific need, the pride with which we wore it the first few times. Seeing something we might not have worn in a while can bring back a wealth of associations: Ah, I wore that to the lake, to the birthday party, on the day I made an important discovery, or met my best friend. Or we see a photo, even years later, and the past becomes present: how that vivid fuchsia or buttery yellow captured my happiness! That was the perfect outfit for that occasion, that weather, those companions. Sometimes fabric can hold fragrance too: the wood smoke lacing the pajamas from a special night in a mountain cabin or a rainy one at home, the perfume or aftershave a loved one wore, their unmistakable presence through their distinctive scent.

By today's standards Dorcas's creations might seem drab and unstylish. But what continues to animate women is that same spark of creativity, channeled now in different ways. Some find a similar craft that engages their urge to create and gives them quiet time. Some channel their artistry into creating a life. Perhaps it was the time spent thinking as she sewed that prepared Dorcas for the message of Jesus. All that time wasn't wasted; it became preparation to welcome his message.

In the hymn "We Come to Your Feast" we sing about "the weaving of our stories, the fabric of our lives." In some rituals parishioners bring forward "the gleaming cloth of white" to place upon the altar, just as they might prepare the dining table at their homes. One of Jesus's great gifts was taking ordinary routines like bathing a baby, sewing a garment, or setting a table and transforming them into carriers of profound meaning, or what some traditions call baptism, Eucharist—a sacrament.

No words can capture the anticipation of pregnancy; the wonder, fear, and awe that surround the birth of a new child. Some of that intense feeling might pour into making booties or quilts or be knitted or crocheted into a blanket. Similarly, we know that a meal can be holy, even an ordinary one at home where we pause to appreciate family members, rest, tell stories, laugh, and refuel. Jesus lifted that relaxed intimacy to another plane when he gave his body and blood at the last supper, saying, "Remember me." If *this* meal is holy, he was saying, so are *all* meals.

Some might affectionately call Dorcas a "church lady." While few parishes still have Dorcas sewing circles, other groups have taken their place and still offer community for many women. We all recognize the female leaders without whom many communities would fall apart in no time. While caring for their own families, they also run educational programs for children and adults, organize the care of the poor, manage outreach to countless fine projects, lead workshops and retreats, spearhead Bible study and prayer services, collect clothing and food, fill and direct choirs, study civic and religious issues, provide spiritual direction, decorate the church, observe birthdays and feasts, drive the elderly, visit the hospitalized, sensitize us to the environmental impacts of our choices, cook meals after funerals. No wonder they're tired!

Scripture scholar Barbara Reid underscores the importance of such women to the early Christian community. Dorcas's name is the only time in the New Testament that the title "disciple" is attached to a single individual, meaning "she taught" or "she follows the ways of Jesus." The verb meaning "do good" implies "healing," as Jesus did. The urgency of the disciples' request to Peter—"Come to us without delay!"—shows her importance to the community as the leader of a house church. Her cure takes place in the upper room of a house, where the Jerusalem community also gathered to be revived from grief and fear at Pentecost.[2]

Psychoanalyst Dr. Theodore Rubin cautions against an identity based solely on accomplishment. He debunks the pretense

---

[2] Barbara Reid, *Taking Up the Cross* (Minneapolis: Augsburg Fortress, 2007), 150–51.

of being always "self-sacrificing and saintlike." He writes, "The concept of good and bad people is a simplistic cultural concept with no basis in reality." Anything that appears to be a failure for heroic types can disrupt the personality's fragile balance and lead to depression. When Rubin experienced this personally, he couldn't sleep until with the help of his wife and analyst, he finally decided to "simply let go, relax, stop berating myself, stop attempting to be in charge . . . to let be what would be."[3] This shift in attitude led to humility, compassion, and a peaceful sleep. Sounds similar to Dorcas's process.

The way Acts describes Dorcas—"devoted to good deeds and acts of charity"—could set off a warning bell. To constantly be the nice guy or gal imposes an inhuman burden on anyone. After her long sleep Dorcas woke to a more realistic sense of herself. She may also have realized how short and precarious life is, and from that perspective, decided to focus her activities more on those that brought joy. All people are composed of virtues and flaws, achievements and failures in a mixture that we deny at our peril. Accepting that *we're* not perfect leads to greater self-compassion and patient understanding of others. And apparently God loves us just the way we are!

QUESTIONS FOR REFLECTION AND DISCUSSION

1. If you thought back over your life as Dorcas does in her "sleep," seeing different articles of clothing to represent each phase, what would be the highlights? Are there any garments you especially remember? Why?

2. If you were one of Dorcas's friends who stood weeping beside Peter in Acts 9:39, what would you say to her as she awoke?

3. Sometimes it takes serious illness to get our attention. What have you learned from illness and/or healing, your own or a loved one's?

---

[3] Theodore Rubin, *Compassion and Self-Hate* (New York: Ballantine Books, 1975), 142, 205, 4.

4. Do you ever feel as exhausted as Dorcas did, not only physically but also emotionally or spiritually? Describe that condition. Have you learned to strike a balance between being and doing? If so, how? If not, describe someone you admire who has found this balance.

5. Have you struggled with perfectionism, which Rubin calls a "ruinous hoax"[4] destructive to normal, limited, fallible human happiness? If so, describe it. Have you come to a resolution about it?

6. Does your parish or community adequately recognize the contribution of women? If so, how? If not, how could that change?

[4] Rubin, 142.

23

Phoebe and Friends

(Romans 16:1–2)

I simply did what needed doing.

My dear friend Paul commended me for my deacon's work in the church of Cenchreae, the one mention of me that's endured. But we had none of the titles that must have evolved later. I wanted to bear witness to Jesus, to follow him, and to do his work. You might say he captured my imagination; he became my great happiness.

Anyone who heard him for more than a day or two knew his focus on letting go of nonessentials. To him, those "fields shining white for the harvest" were more compelling than any synagogue authorities. After all, the man was baptized in a river by a fellow who ate locusts! No formal ritual in the temple for *his* initiation rite. None of the trappings of tribalism for him! Did he ever ask anyone for a marriage license or a baptismal certificate before he cured them? Did he check up on what church they attended or quiz them on purity codes before they had a conversation?

We tried to shape our priorities like those of Jesus. I was Paul's coworker, and we had much to do—even if some of my influence was reining in his large ego and toning down his zeal! I didn't even object to his description of me: "a benefactor of many and of myself as well" (Acts 16:2).

My hometown, Cenchreae, was Corinth's eastern seaport, a place of crosscurrents where cultures meet and stories spread. A good place to be! I had managed a household, raised a family, and welcomed friends to my home. It seemed a natural step to host Christian communities. Why would I suddenly take a lesser role? Paul certainly wasn't threatened by me; indeed he welcomed and appreciated all the gifts everyone brought to his magnificent enterprise.[1] We may have been small groups of only forty or so, but we knew we could make tremendous change in the ego-driven, power-hungry, slaveholding society in which we lived.

All that may explain why, when Paul asked me to carry his letter, I said, "Of course!" I had the means and the wit; I liked adventure and liked carrying good news—why not? What an honor to read his message aloud for the first time.

I may get the press, but I wasn't the only one. A tomb inscription in Cappadocia describes the less glorious work of more anonymous women: "Here lies the deacon Maria . . . who according to the words of the apostle raised children, sheltered guests, washed the feet of the saints, and shared her bread with the needy."[2]

I'd be honored to stand as a representative of so many women, unnamed and unsung, who built that early church, pulled between arguments and grace. There are tantalizing mentions of some women in Acts. What about Philip's four unmarried daughters who had the gift of prophecy? (Acts 21:8–11). Had they been men, they surely would have been given more than a fleeting reference. Perhaps, following in their father's footsteps, they brought their gifts to Caesarea's Christians.

We know so little of the slave-girl "who had a spirit of divination," not even her name (Acts 16:16–24). Ironic how, when she followed Paul and other disciples, she'd call out, "These men are slaves of the Most High God, who proclaim to you a way of salvation." Anywhere else, she would've been praised as a prophet,

---

[1] Florence Gillman, *Women Who Knew Paul* (Collegeville, MN: Liturgical Press, 1992), 41–42.

[2] Phyllis Zagano, *Holy Saturday* (New York: Crossroad, 2000), 94.

but Paul was annoyed. He drove out the spirit, enraging her owners who saw the end of their moneymaking scheme. No more profits from her fortune-telling, so they dragged Paul, Silas, and others before magistrates and had them flogged and imprisoned. We know the story of their escape, but what of her? She's never mentioned again. Only imagination could concoct her future—possibly initial bewilderment, then perhaps a place in the Christian community? Or a return to the misery of slavery, without the solace of a gift that distinguished her? Her owners might well have taken out their anger—violently—on her.

Or Mary (Acts 12:12), mother of Mark, whose house was a gathering place of disciples in Jerusalem? She was not only a gracious hostess, but she set the tone of prayer. And what of Rhoda, who provides a welcome note of humor to the whole book? I'll let her tell her own story. . . .

RHODA, WHO GAVE PETER PAUSE (ACTS 12:12–17)

I was a maid to Mary, the best job I'd ever had. My parents sold me into work when I was five, and that began a long tunnel of abuse. Maybe a few blows to the head had addled my brain, I don't know. I was just grateful to work for Mary. She never beat me, and these friends of Jesus were usually gentle and forgiving. Oh, they had their crazies and their geniuses, just like any other collection of humans, but I felt more at ease with them than with any group I'd ever met. That's why I didn't want to disappoint them. I was glad they gave me a simple job like opening the door. I felt sure I could do *that*! Or could I?

I'd heard Peter speak only a few times, but he must have been an important leader, the way they carried on and prayed like mad when he got arrested. When I heard banging at the gate, I hated to leave that fervent company. I knew Peter was bound and chained in his cell, so I couldn't believe my eyes, to see him in the dark shadows at the gate, and hear his voice. Indeed, I was so overjoyed, I ran to tell the others, forgetting to let him in! Some told me I was nuts, but I held my ground—I'd recognize that voice anywhere. Meanwhile, Peter patiently continued to knock, a dull thumping that accompanied the incredulous comments and dismissive conversation. Finally, in all the commotion, a few people came back with me and let him in.

They were quick to forgive, these Christians. But what meant the most was when Peter himself drew me aside a few days later and said:

> "You know, Rhoda, I haven't always been the most prayerful, reflective guy. I was more the kind who plunged in first, thought about it later. Even Jesus couldn't change who I am.
>
> "In prison the night before I met you, I'd thought I was doomed. Herod had James killed with a sword. I thought sure I was next, because that whiff of blood and violence 'pleased the people.' When I first encountered Jesus, it was as if a great door swung open into a different world, a way of being so far removed from my usual work of fishing, I felt like another person. Those few years with him were the best of my life; I hated to see them end. In a way, his presence continued with his friends after his death, but I *have* been eager to see him again. So, I slept that night between two soldiers with a sense of finality. The door that had once opened would clang shut the next day—or open on another mysteriously splendid chapter with the Jesus I'd come to love. I had walked with him for several years; now I fully anticipated he'd be at my side as I entered eternity.
>
> "When the *prison* doors and the iron gate of the city swung open, I thought I was dreaming. This wasn't quite the surprise I'd anticipated! Eventually I 'came to myself'—a phrase Jesus was fond of using. I think it's in the story of the prodigal son, which applies to me more than anyone else who heard it. So when I got to Mary's house and knocked, I saw dim lamps and it seemed like another series of gates began to open. Maybe Jesus wasn't quite done with me yet.

"Even though I was tired that night, as I waited for you to return, wondering *if* you'd return, it gave me a chance to think. I remembered another serving girl who recognized my speech. It seemed a long time ago, that other confrontation, but the raw pain still felt fresh. How miserably I'd failed when the girl in the courtyard outside Caiaphas's palace said, 'Your speech betrays you. You are a Galilean.' You may not know this, but I denied Jesus—not only once, but three times! If I could be forgiven *that* betrayal, nothing else mattered much. I'd trust whatever door swung open next. That reminds me, didn't Jesus once say he was the gate? And what about, 'seek and you will find; knock and the door will be opened to you'? It seemed like you were gone a long time, but the memories kept me company as I wrapped my cloak close in the night chill.

"I'll always remember the sight of your lantern returning to the gate, at first just a distant, bouncy glow, but growing brighter as you approached. I'll use that image, I think, if I ever get around to writing. Maybe good news comes to us like that too, first blurry, then an intense light."

I was just a maid, but this important man was telling me how *he'd* failed! And *his* betrayal made my blunder look small. Maybe I was silly, easily distracted, and unfocused, but all of us are flawed somehow, and that is OK. Once I would've been beaten mercilessly if a boss knew I hadn't opened the door to an honored guest. Now, I was hearing that the big leader had made plenty of mistakes himself!

AVA, AN UNWILLING CONVERT (ACTS 16:22–34)

Now *here's* a story we don't hear much about. . . .

I wasn't consulted about my conversion. Hearing that dynamite word, you might think of an inner shift or a surge of spirit. Nope. My husband, Brutus, gave the impulsive order, "Baptize my whole household!" Someone I'd never met named Paul sprinkled water, said some words, and that was it. Only later would I understand.

Brutus was a jailer. As you can imagine, our conversations were perfunctory—a few grunts now and then, but not many chatty topics in his line of work. Until that day.

He told the story so often, I knew it by heart. The usual brutality for the prisoners; the magistrates had warned that these two were especially dangerous. So Brutus chained their feet to a stake. Duty done, he had a few drinks with his buddies and then fell asleep despite the annoying songs and prayers.

But an earthquake jolted them awake. Floors shook violently, and doors flew open. Brutus, seeing the commotion and assuming the prisoners had taken an easy out, drew his sword to kill himself. (He probably figured that would be a better end than the torturous deaths he'd seen magistrates devise and Romans inflict.) But a voice stopped him; in utter disbelief he rushed to the source and found the prisoners alive, choking in the dust just as he was.

Apparently that sent Brutus right over the top; he fell to the ground and begged for salvation. Next thing I knew, I was awakened in the middle of the night and told to bring water and towels for the red welts swelling on Paul's and Silas's legs and feet. Then, orders for the servants to prepare a feast—at 3:00 a.m.

After the drama of that night, baptism seemed minor. But since then I've had more time to think. What kind of crazy prisoner saves his jailer? Wouldn't anyone in jail seize the chance to be vindictive and rid himself of an enemy? Paul and Silas could've scooted right out the open door, but they stayed to reassure Brutus. The two prisoners seemed equally flummoxed, all humans staring in the same bewilderment as their jailers at crumbled walls, fallen stones, and iron chains suddenly tangled like yarn in a sewing basket. Some power greater than the Roman Empire was at work here, and if I wanted to save my skin, I'd align with it too.

What had begun as self-preservation turned into something more. We met some other Christians and liked them. We were there to hear Paul's letter to the community at Philippi. How odd that his former jailer was in the crowd, which had now become dear to him. But if I've learned anything from this crew, it's that things get overturned and surprises happen, and that an earthquake seems the *least* of it. That was just the beginning!

PHOEBE AND FRIENDS TODAY

Despite few materials about or *by* women from the early Christian era, "we should make creative use of what we have."[3] We know that Phoebe was a woman of wealth and power, probably the bearer of the Letter to the Romans, a teacher and a benefactor.[4] Paul calls her "deacon," a term he uses for coworkers, servants, and ministers "on a par with him and the men."[5] Simply the lack of knowledge about these women doesn't mean giving up on them. For that would mean "letting those who have erased women from history have the last say."[6]

A total of nine women named in the Letter to the Romans suggests an egalitarian movement with women in positions of authority. Oddly enough, their roles may have been dictated by social norms. For example, a man couldn't touch a woman during a baptismal anointing or visit a woman alone—hence, women into the breach! Any discussion of ordinations and hierarchies would have bewildered them, since Jesus ordained no one. Like any healthy family or community, they simply responded generously to the immediate needs, not concerned with titles or status.

Phoebe stands as one whose role was eminently practical, like those who offered their homes for meeting places of the fledgling

---

[3] Elizabeth Clark, "Early Christian Women: Sources and Interpretation," in *That Gentle Strength: Historical Perspectives on Women in Christianity*, ed. Lynda Coon et al.(Charlottesville: University Press of Virginia, 1990), 19.

[4] Carol Newsome and Sharon Ringe, eds., *The Women's Bible Commentary* (Louisville, KY: Westminster/John Knox Press, 1992), 320.

[5] Gillman, *Women Who Knew Paul*, 62–63.

[6] Bernadette Brooten, quoted in Gillman, 15.

community. The Christian tradition has always upheld both its pragmatists and its mystics; some women saints like Hildegard of Bingen and Teresa of Avila were both. "Paul would be the first to welcome all attempts to portray these women in their own right since for many of them . . . he expressed praise and gratitude."[7]

By the late first or early second century some parts of the church tried to tone down places in Acts showing women being an important part of the early Christian community.[8] Scholars like William Ramsay noted long ago that the church had to blend in with Roman society, which held women in low esteem, and would look askance at the prominence of women in this new sect.

Given this background, let's try to make a small comparison of the early church with our churches today.

A woman, whom we'll name Barbara, who had faithfully served her parish in many capacities, including pastoral associate, helping a priest with Alzheimer's disease, had encouraged beautiful liturgical traditions and lay homilists. The community took strong stands for social justice, opened a food bank, and offered sessions to inform immigrants of their rights. But her hard work fell apart when a new pastor returned the place to the fifties, defending "how the church has always been." No more lay involvement, meaningful homilies, or beautiful creative liturgies. Many people left; others remain, disgruntled. The church building itself is a huge cavern, half filled; people cringe at the "hellfire and brimstone" homilies.

And Barbara? She sings in the choir, grateful she's not responsible if anything goes haywire. She doesn't seem angry or bitter, invests most of her time in her grandchildren, and says, "Thirty years ago, there was such a resurgence of enthusiasm for parish ministry. Women were getting degrees and jobs; they began to feel empowered. Now it seems to have vanished. For most of the people I know who worked in parishes, it ended badly."

---

[7] Gillman, 91.

[8] Ben Witherington, quoted in Gillman, 26.

Two religious women concur; their communities don't waste time placing highly educated members in parishes. With rare exceptions they dread the twenty-something pastors with no experience who will quickly "put sister in her place." The pay is abysmal; the sisters would rather put their energies where they'll be more appreciated. African American theologian Sister Jamie Phelps adds: "I'm not saying that everybody needs to preach. But there are gifts out there that are not being recognized, not being nurtured, not being used to continue the mission of Jesus Christ."[9]

Into this sad situation the words of Sister Joan Chittister come as a clarion call:

> Indeed, when the Church and its documents and its structures and its symbols and its language and its laws and its liturgies forgets or forgoes or forswears the place of women in the Christian dispensation, there in its Scriptures the vision of Jesus with women stays vibrant and vital and unable to be forgotten. And without it, so much poorer the Church.[10]

QUESTIONS FOR REFLECTION AND DISCUSSION

1. Women wouldn't radically alter the person they'd been—"active and decisive leaders within their own spheres of concern"—as Florence Gillman points out,[11] simply because they became Christian. So they were key influences in the early church.

Similarly, women supported Saint Ignatius Loyola from the earliest days of his uncertain path toward writing the *Spiritual*

[9] Jamie Phelps, OP, quoted in Michael O'Loughlin, "Want to See Catholic Women Preach? Soon You'll Be Able To," *America* (October 27, 2016).

[10] Joan Chittister, "What's Right with the Catholic Church?" in *WomanStrength: Modern Church, Modern Women* (Kansas City, MO: Sheed and Ward, 1990), 45.

[11] Gillman, *Women Who Knew Paul*, 91.

Exercises and founding the Society of Jesus. Not only did they provide practical housing and finances, they told him to clean up his act, quit the extreme fasting, trim his overgrown beard, and dress better if he wanted people to take him seriously.

It's easy to see women's effects historically, as in these two examples, but often harder to see them today. Is Barbara's experience above typical? Where do you see hope for women in the church? What gifts do you see women bringing your church community today? Where are you disappointed? Are women's contributions today more obvious in the arenas of government, business, technology, education, the arts, science, and medicine than in the church? If so, where? in what ways are you heartened by this larger arena ?

2. After her experience neglecting Peter, Rhoda probably thought a lot about doors. (Peter also had a chance to reflect on the meaning of gates and doors.) They fill our days too: the first threshold of the morning into the new day, the last tired trudge at night through the doors of home. A family approaching its vacation cottage every summer unlocks the door with high excitement, anticipating relaxation, laughter, play, meals, and time together. They lock it after a week or so with fulfillment and sadness—it will be a whole year before they come together again in that way. Sometimes we stare hard at a closed door, waiting for someone we've missed a long time to reappear or an opportunity to arise. Sometimes that door never opens. Sadly, the door of the hospital room, funeral home, or morgue closes with a dreadful finality. Sometimes a door we once thought permanently slammed shut reopens or gives us a glimpse through a crack.

What doors do you open and close daily? Have you ever thought about their significance? If you do, what surfaces? Over the course of a lifetime what doors and subsequent paths have molded and shaped you?

3. Another image that's significant in the story is the lantern Rhoda must've used to make her way to the gate—twice. It's interesting to speculate whether Peter might've remembered it and used it when he wrote: "So we have the prophetic message more

fully confirmed. You will do well to be attentive to this as to a lamp shining in a dark place, until the day dawns and the morning star rises in your hearts" (2 Pet 1:19). Although scholars say that the author of this letter probably wasn't Peter himself, using his name was an accepted way of honoring him. "The use of an apostle's name in reasserting his teaching was not regarded as dishonest but was merely a way of reminding the church of what it had received from God through that apostle."[12] The image remains powerful, especially now, when neuroscientists tell us we can change our customary, negative "thought ruts" by directing them into more positive channels. In that sense, "lamps shining in dark places" can lift our sights from draining frustration or evil realities to a better place.

What are the bright lights for you? Does focusing on them help you avoid negativity? What do you think the "morning star rising in your heart" might mean?

4. After Rhoda's great gaffe, Peter speaks of his own terrible betrayal. What a gift that a leader of the early Christian community had made some terrible mistakes and wasn't afraid to admit it! This exchange reflects the wisdom of Henri Nouwen:

> Mostly we are so afraid of our weaknesses that we hide them at all cost and thus make them unavailable to others but also often to ourselves. And, in this way, we end up living double lives even against our own desires: one life in which we present ourselves to the world, to ourselves, and to God as a person who is in control and another life in which we feel insecure, doubtful, confused, and anxious and totally out of control. . . .
>
> It is amazing in my own life that true friendship and community became possible to the degree that I was able to share my weaknesses with others. Often I became aware

---

[12] "The Second Letter of Peter," in *The New Oxford Annotated Bible*, ed. Bruce Metzger and Roland Murphy (New York: Oxford University Press, 1991), 344NT.

> of the fact that in the sharing of my weaknesses with others, the real depths of my human brokenness and weakness and sinfulness started to reveal themselves to me, not as a source of despair but as a source of hope. As long as I try to convince myself or others of my independence, a lot of my energy is invested in building up my own false self. But once I am able to truly confess my most profound dependence on others and on God, I can come in touch with my true self and real community can develop.[13]

Do you agree with Nouwen? Have you been able to share your own weaknesses and human limitations, or is that challenge still down the road?

5. Ava didn't agree to her conversion and was roped into baptism by her husband. But it's possible it turned out well. She seems to lean toward appreciating the long-range effects of that earthquake.

Have you ever had second, more positive thoughts about some action you undertook reluctantly? Or, were you ever coerced into a decision (for instance, about a school choice, a move, a relationship, a job shift) that initially seemed wrong, then led to some unexpected blessing?

---

[13] Henri J. M. Nouwen, *You Are the Beloved* (New York: Convergent, 2017), 227.

Questions to Conclude Parts I–III

1. Explore the New Testament and find a woman you're curious about, one whose story, actions, and ideas we don't know. Using a Midrash technique, recreate her imaginatively. (It's possible she's simply one of a crowd, a bystander at a miracle, a woman who never met Jesus but was curious about him. How did he affect her life—or not?) How does the Midrash technique work for you?

2. In the course of this book we've seen how different women met Jesus, interacted with him, and continued (or didn't) the relationship. These are only a handful of the women who've followed him over the centuries, each path unique. But their stories are useful as stepping stones to ours. Let's look now at our personal stories:

- In one sentence, summarize the effect you see Jesus having on the women in this book.
- List or name mentally ten adjectives that describe your relationship with Jesus.
- How do you feel that relationship has changed in the last ten years? Twenty? Or for some, fifty? How has it changed since you began reading this book?
- What have been the most significant effects on the relationship?
- Where would you like to see this relationship go next?

PART IV

GROUP RESOURCES

The following monologues could be part of a dramatic presentation during a worship service or used as the prayer for a small group or retreat. All except the first, The Samaritan Woman, appear in longer form in the earlier parts of this book, but people who are hearing them rather than reading them will appreciate the shorter texts. Creative leaders will find other occasions to use them and may benefit from reading the longer stories and considering the Questions for Reflection and Discussion that follow them. Invite those doing the reading to look over the monologue before presenting it to the group.

The Samaritan Woman Speaks

(John 4:1–42)

The Samaritan woman is not "hidden"—her story is widely known—so there is not a longer chapter about her in this book. Nonetheless, this monologue might be helpful for church services in Lent, when her story is read, in personalizing her viewpoint.

I just wanted to fill my bucket and get home before it got any hotter. But that plan got derailed by the most marvelous conversation. I wanted to tell the stranger, "You must be new around here. Jewish men don't talk to Samaritan women in public." Or, "Look, pal. I gotta get home. The man I live with wants his water!"

Instead, I got pulled into this amazing discussion. This wandering teacher took me seriously. He didn't dismiss my desires as everyone else would—dangerous unless controlled by men! In fact, he never got his drink, and I never filled my bucket. We set aside our pressing projects, our differences with our churches and each other for a short time—and whoosh! "Water gushing up to everlasting life!"

I guess he liked my nerve. After all, I've broken all the social taboos—what have I got to lose? Maybe you could say I was open to his message. And I liked the way he *invited*—never coerced. My life was pretty topsy-turvy anyway; I was used to surprises. He probed my past, but not in a scrutinizing way. Somehow, he led me from talking about ordinary water to another plane altogether.

I used to think the lines between Jews and Samaritans were as rigid as walls. After all, everyone in my world regarded them as high barriers. But this guy didn't seem to care; he dismissed big differences easy as fluff on the wind. He reminded me of the prophets—like Amos or Micah or Isaiah, focused on the important things, trying to direct me away from the trivia. You could say that I'd already stepped out of religious circles or that they had scorned me. Maybe that's why I responded to him so fast; at some level, I already knew what he was saying. Much later, I remembered his phrase, "If you knew the gift of God." Well maybe I do. Or I'm learning.

As we talked, I glimpsed something deep within myself, a depth I never knew I had. It was that spark within that responded to his promise. He made me feel happy, dignified—as I had never felt before. Many don't notice an important sentence in my story: "Then the woman left her water jar." No more defining *my* life by domestic drudgery! Now I know I'm cut out for something else. It's rumored that years later women left their jars filled with embalming spices at an empty tomb. They too found more important things to do, like witness a resurrection.

Remember how I came to the well—alone, at the hottest time, when no one else would be there, avoiding the gossips and judges? That all changed. I ran back to my village as loud as a brass band. No longer ashamed, I was so caught up in astonishment that I could trumpet, "He told me everything I've ever done!" Suddenly I felt strong, like a precious vessel spilling over with good news. Bursting, I began to tell the town.

QUESTIONS FOR REFLECTION AND DISCUSSION

1. With her lively spontaneity and enthusiastic initiative the Samaritan woman could serve as a bridge between the ancient text and women today who are much like her. What role could you see her taking if she lived now (elected official, CEO of an international nonprofit, pope, hospice nurse, philosophy professor, . . .)?

2. If you could audition favorite movie stars to play the role of the Samaritan woman, whom would you invite? Who might come closest to capturing her *attitude*? How would you costume her?

3. Despite the discomfort of the male disciples, Jesus vindicates the woman, suggesting that she participates in the harvest of ripe "fruit for eternal life" (Jn 4:36). Name one of your own achievements in which Jesus takes delight.

4. What good news do you hesitate to share? For what bold grace might you ask the Samaritan woman?

Chloe, a Servant at Cana, Speaks

(John 2:1–11)

In my world being a woman *and* a servant was the double whammy. Long, exhausting days faded numbingly into each other, each identical to the last. No wonder we anticipated a wedding, even though it meant more work. At a wedding banquet, people who never feasted got to eat more than they'd ever dreamed. Even we servants sneaked more food. From a meager diet, we plunged into seven days of eating. For once, we all felt full.

Filling the six heavy stone jars with water was backbreaking. I heard an earnest woman's voice but dismissed it as just one more crisis, another command, when we already had too much to do.

But then I thought, *crazy*. I'm getting too tired. It looked as if the water had a burgundy sheen, as though the gray stone were tinted. The steward was clueless as always. My aching arms were stiff, but crazy-hopeful, I lifted a ladle. That unexpected wine surpassed anything I'd ever tasted!

Sipping it, I understood for the first time what the rabbis had always taught. Marriage is a symbol of the relationship between Israel and God. But with delight filling my mouth, I thought: God chose me. From the beginning of time, God sought me like a bride. Always, God's compassion has reached toward me. Words couldn't capture my awe, but burgundy could. An odd intoxication that lasted long. Life afterward could be dull again, grueling hand-to-mouth survival. But I would carry that taste within.

Then, when I thought I might be getting used to this radical about-face, a friend told me a story from that same wedding guest, Jesus. He shocked people when he told the story of *servants being served*.

This Jesus seemed to have an odd affinity with us bottom-of-the-heap sorts. A master acting as a servant? Maybe it's not so startling. This guy Jesus also said only the "little ones" get it. Couldn't get much littler than me!

Zacchaeus's Daughter Speaks

(LUKE 19:1–10)

My dad taught me to climb trees, and not many girls did *that* in Jericho. Sycamores were his favorite; he'd show me the knotty handholds. Once we were swaying at the top, he'd sweep the horizon with one open hand. "Box seats on the whole town, sweetie!" I'd grin back at him and feel like I was queen of the world. From my leafy perch I ruled with kind nobility, tall and true. And he would be my king. Later, I'd appreciate his giving me a spunk my friends didn't have.

I was his only daughter, so I could wheedle, "Daddy, which dress should I get, the red or the blue?" I knew exactly what he'd say: "Aw, darlin' . . . get both!" He delighted in bringing me gifts: maybe a scarf the blue-lavender shades of the ocean, or candy from another country. By the time I was twelve, I stood as tall as he. We'd play like buddies together, tuning out any disapproving clucks about the bark in our hair or the scrapes on our shins.

But as I grew older, I noticed grumbling. People hated daddy's profession and his wealth. Probably because they were scraping to eat regularly, we, by contrast, seemed too carefree in our high balcony of branches. But swaying there, imagining I could touch the clouds, I didn't much care.

Of course, dad took me with him the day that Jesus entered town. He never wanted me to miss anything, so we ran ahead of the crowd like lookouts, gasping and flushed. I had scrambled up the tree beside dad when suddenly I glimpsed an upturned chin. Even better: the face below us was *grinning* and inviting himself to our house.

My dad scrambled down that tree, for the first time leaving me to fend for myself. Good thing I'd shinnied down trees before! I overheard dad say something about giving to the poor, which didn't surprise me. He'd always opened his purse to just about anyone who'd ask. I couldn't complain. I'd received so many of his gifts, why not share the bounty?

My dad was usually exuberant, but with his guest alongside, he danced toward home. I was doing a little jig myself, trying to keep up and eavesdrop. My dad always enjoyed a good joke, and this fellow was matching him with riddles and stories that left them both howling. Meanwhile, the crowd kept up the criticism, pecking at dad like chickens at grain. But he wouldn't let their small-minded comments stain his joy.

Closing the door of our home firmly on the gossips outside, Dad broke out the best wine—how *else* to celebrate such an uninvited, honored guest? While he and his guest exchanged toasts, I scurried to the kitchen, dreading what I'd find. As I'd guessed, my mother was flummoxed, whispering: "No one told *me* about dinner guests! I *had* enough lamb and bread for the three of us, then unannounced, another hungry person appears at the door!"

But I liked this surprise guest, because he had the same lilting laughter as my dad. So I didn't mind helping to prepare a meal. Who *else* would run next door to borrow more food? The stranger breathed deep of the roasting fragrance and complimented *both* mom and me. To him, I wasn't the annoying kid. I was the princess who ruled with wisdom and grace. I wonder if he's also a tree climber.

The Mother Who Brought Her Child to Jesus Speaks

(Mark 10:13–16; Matthew 18:1–5, 19:13–15)

My daughter Hannah grew up happy, cuddly, eagerly lifting her head to see what was new. Her radiant smile beamed like a shaft of sunlight in fog. Always, I shielded her, fearing where her curiosity might lead. Never too far away, I protected every move. I worried that even the bright flax of her hair in sunlight might attract danger.

Then one day while we were out for our walk, her hand safe in mine, we heard a commotion. Other mothers with their children were crowding around some man. I didn't want to miss out. Could a girl child come too? As I edged forward, I heard harsh words from other men trying to drive us away. I've experienced enough of that discouragement to last a lifetime, so I tried to distract Hannah and turned in another direction.

But she was stubborn, like her mother. She insisted on plunging forward to investigate. Nothing, not even my strong arms, could restrain her. Soon I heard loud indignation and feared for her safety. Astonishing, though. The speaker was rebuking his friends, inviting the children, not sending them away.

Hannah was drawn to the kind voice; I couldn't prevent her lurching toward him. The next thing I knew, she was scooped into his arms, round as a bowl. He hugged her and blessed her as I have done every day of her life. The gesture must have seemed familiar, intimate. She didn't struggle beneath his hands or wail for me as I'd expected. Instead, she cupped his chin in her tiny hand and traced his eyebrow with one plump finger.

It was tempting to tell her father, triumphant. But that night I heard Hannah humming herself to sleep, utterly content and self-contained. Maybe she didn't need that time with the teacher, but I did. The reassurance he extended to her found a home in me. I could've easily been the unsure girl who scrambled into the big hug just to hear, "You're OK." More than OK, but my words couldn't stretch large enough to hold that abundance. It was as if all the colors of sunset spilled into me, crimson and fuchsia and saffron.

I knew then that the lovely image of Hannah with the teacher was a secret to hold close to my heart. It was almost as if he'd shown me the feminine face of God, Sophia. When I pray for Hannah now, I say to God, "as one mother to another." After that day, I've lived with a confidence, a certainty I never had before. Neither she nor I was God's afterthought, an inferior species. Even better, Jesus had told Hannah the kingdom of heaven was *hers*.

The Woman Who Lost the Coin Speaks

(LUKE 15:8–10, 21:1–4)

I couldn't manage money, but I excelled at parties. It all began when I was a young mother. I remember Jesus watching that day as I burrowed through the muck on the floor, desperate to find that coin. Of all my son's friends, he was the most thoughtful, slightly more serious than the other boys. They were all so young then, absorbed in play. Most of them barely noticed my dilemma. But Jesus was different. It was as if he stored my experience in some quiet trove that he'd bring forth years later.

But as I said, I wasn't paying much attention to him. I needed that coin badly, and my only form of safekeeping had failed. Back then, we were desperately poor, and that coin meant meals for the family. I berated myself as I hunted and swept: how could I be so careless?

When I finally heard the clink against the broom, I let out a hoot that the children could hear outdoors. I grasped it tightly in my fist as I danced around our little home, exuberant. But what's good news without girlfriends? *This* was the time to celebrate. Word spreads quickly through my neighborhood, and soon we collected a few treats the children rarely have, a little wine for the adults, and presto! A party.

Jesus was part of it all, solemnly chewing his sweet with the other children. I gave it little thought afterward. But that joy continued to fill me, brimming over with the coppery glow of an inner treasure.

Twenty years later I'd learned I couldn't control everything. That found coin I clenched so close was quickly spent, as were others that followed. Maybe as I aged I relaxed more with money as with everything else. One day, I agreed when a friend wanted me to hear the new wandering preacher in town. She'd been so kind, it seemed like a small thing to accompany her that day.

Oddly enough, this rabbi didn't speak in the synagogue. I was glad I could hear him outdoors, in the open air, without all the stifling male ritual.

You can imagine my astonishment when he spoke of something so familiar, so close to home, it seemed to rise up from within me. "Or what woman having ten coins and losing one . . . " Suddenly, I was young again, desperately lighting a lamp and peering into the dusty corners.

I pushed forward to look more closely at the speaker. How could he have known my story? Then I heard his name. Jesus had been there for the loss and the finding, the party that followed. From my frustration he carved a parable. I was at my worst that day, but he made me a figure of God.

So the joy continued afterward. I always remembered how *my* lost coin showed God seeking out the lost ones. If God were as persistent as I had been, how could I not feel secure? Not only was the coin found: *I* was too! It was almost as if I knew God from within, as closely as one of my friends. A few women had gone through it all with me: the marriages and births, the tragedies and celebrations, the illnesses and deaths. Imagine that: God as close as one of these companions! The rabbis had never told me that. But I knew that the only way it counts—firsthand.

Parties were rare in our village, and maybe we enjoyed them more because they didn't come often. But after I heard Jesus's parable, I understood; the party is within me.

The Foolish Bridesmaid Speaks

(Matthew 25:1–13)

For centuries I've been called foolish. But you haven't heard my side of the story.

When my cousin Esther asked me to be part of her wedding party, I twirled with excitement. It was as if she had offered me the key to another country.

It was hard to understand marriage, because my parents detested each other. Often the last noise I heard before falling asleep was my father beating my mother and her frightened, muffled cry. Her bruises in the morning were pitiful, but even worse was her attempt to hide them and protect him. When I caught the scent of something different in *this* wedding, I paid attention.

Esther's groom, Mical, wasn't handsome; in fact, he was pudgy. But he treated her like his dearest friend. When he wanted another opinion, he didn't just ask his male friends; *her* vote mattered. They laughed together often; they walked with the same rhythm. He touched her with tenderness, and she shimmered. His voice was gentle; I couldn't imagine him yelling like my father. Cool soup or moldy bread threw dad into a tirade that made me flee the house. But Mical was kind, even to me, the snotty-nosed young cousin with the bad haircut. I guess I was secretly in love with him—all the bridesmaids were. In his company we all felt beautiful and cherished, because we were important to Esther.

Since I'd never been in a wedding, I didn't know about bringing extra oil. We'd all dozed off that night, until my sister poked me, demanding my lamp. Half awake, I gave it to her grudgingly. They say when I was small, I'd toddle around behind her, repeating everything she said. I adored my big sister. I tried to imitate her actions, and surely she knew this wedding business better than I did. So I was puzzled when she told me to go buy more oil. Was this job foisted on the youngest? And where could I get it at midnight?

Into my confusion gradually came one painful truth. I'd be locked out of the banquet. For months I'd fantasized about that feast. I would imagine *that* world whenever my parents nipped at each other or the food on our table was scarce. I would wear a special gown and eat the choicest meal. I might even dance with the groom. Guess I was so hungry for that wedding that losing it felt like a blow to the stomach.

So I wept outside the hall. I could hear the distant music; I could picture Mical looking deep with care into Esther's eyes. No one rescued me; there was no magic ending to the story.

Several years later the old sadness had been somewhat resolved. Then I heard a man named Jesus tell my story, but he'd given it a new twist. "The kingdom of heaven," whatever that meant, would be like the feast I'd missed. That snagged my attention. Would I get a second chance? Could I finally sail, erect and gracious, through that door that once was locked? But the next part made the hair on the back of my neck prickle. God, in the story, was like Mical. That call I'd heard in my sleep could come again: "Behold the bridegroom! Come out to meet him!"

He seemed to be saying that God, like Mical was gentle, brimming with life and joy, energized by Esther's presence. Could God still look tenderly on me, who had failed so miserably to be a wise bridesmaid?

For years I'd been taught that God was like my father, so I wanted to escape. But *this* new comparison gleams with possibility! No more sleeping on the job; this is a God I want to run and meet. *This* God is bride and groom, wine and feast, lamp and friend, wedding and joy.

Next time, I'll be ready.

The Persistent Widow Speaks

(Luke 18:1–8)

Scripture shows the vast complexity of human beings, where no one is 100 percent evil or 100 percent good. Your group may want to stage this as a courtroom drama, with roles for the widow, the judge (in Jesus's day, definitely male; in our day, possibly female), the current landowner, attorneys, and a bailiff in case it gets rowdy. If people worry that scripture is sacrosanct and not to be toyed with, remind them that this comes from a parable, a story Jesus made up. He'd probably be pleased to see you embroider or modernize it.

You'd be persistent too. My neighbor had so blatantly taken my land when my husband died, I was outraged for years. He'd done it cunningly, sneaking in while I was still in shock. Between the blurry edges of grief, I heard his offer, which sounded so generous. He'd "look after things" until I got on my feet. My daughters lived far away; I had no brother. Since few hands were offered in help, I desperately grabbed the one that seemed lifesaving. Stupid and weak, I agreed to his plan. Little did I know that this was his slimy way of encroaching on what was rightly mine.

By the time I realized clearly what had happened, that snake had all the right words to defend his theft: "I was only looking out for your good." "Of course, you understand why, after so much time, it's mine now." And the line that finally drove me to the judge: "No court in the land would pay attention to you, little woman." Of course, he was right. Women counted for less than oxen in my world, and the judge dismissed me more times than I can count.

The anger burned bright enough to fuel my search for justice. No matter how often that judge "patted me on the head" and told me to get lost, I would return. I had no weapon but stubbornness and the conviction that my cause was just. The judge finally told me he was "acting on my behalf"—what would *I* know about managing land?

"Precious little," I'd have said if I answered truthfully. But I wouldn't give him even the slightest doubt, a chink in my armor. I smile when I recall how gradually I wore him down. It even surprises me to see how annoying I became, I who was once well behaved. There were days when I'd tire of the trek to see the judge again. But then I'd think, "What am I doing that's more important?" Or I'd see our land in an afternoon slant of light, radiant with new green shoots. Or I'd remember my husband's pride as he bought one tiny parcel after another, hoping he'd enrich my old age.

Then I'd roar like a mother bear protecting her cubs, and set off again. Each time the judge saw me coming, he probably groaned and sent out the gatekeepers to protect himself. But even they came around to my side, maybe remembering a mother or sister who'd also been abandoned. They'd smuggle me in, and it was a hoot to see his face crumple at the sight of me—again.

I don't know what persuaded him, but one day he capitulated. Maybe he feared I'd grow violent. Maybe he was just exhausted. Maybe he saw an easier way to line his slick pocket. But it didn't matter why or how. All that matters is that I sit on my porch, admire our land, remember my husband, and whisper, "I've kept it, dear."

Lydia Speaks

(Acts 16:14, 40)

You might invite one woman to play Lydia of the New Testament and another woman to represent our contemporary world. One can interview the other or engage in dialogue with her about their work: how it has changed, what concerns stay similar, and so on. If you have extra time to prepare, furnish the women with props such as a purple cloth and an iPhone. "Lydia," for example, might ask the contemporary woman why she's so obsessed with the small, handheld device she carries everywhere. The latter might respond, "Look what this iPhone could do for your dyeing business!"

"I am confident of this, that the one who began a good work among you will bring it to completion by the day of Jesus Christ" (Phil 1:6).

Did you ever wonder who Paul had in mind when he wrote these inspiring words? It was I. I'd long been a successful businesswoman, but this was the culmination of my career. I led the house church that first heard the Letter to the Philippians.

But that gets ahead of my story. Some time earlier I'd gone, as usual, to the river outside the city gate with some friends; it was restful there after a hot day. The green shade was peaceful beside the stream after the noise of the marketplace. We were sitting with our feet in cool water, talking quietly, when Paul and Silas arrived. It began as a chance (or graced) encounter and eventually led to Paul describing us as "my brothers and sisters whom I love and long for, my joy and crown" (Phil 4:1). You must be wondering what happened in between.

My town, Philippi, was a bustling place, located on the Greco-Roman trade routes. I was a successful merchant; I sold my finest textiles to wealthy Romans. But being "a dealer in purple cloth" wasn't enough. I thirsted for more. Paul's message spilled into my thirsty spirit like the waters of that stream.

Really, I "needed nothing from him," being financially secure with an established business. But I had to challenge him to make sure there'd be no more social inequality with these Christians. So I said, "If you have judged me to be faithful to the Lord, come and stay at my home."

Guess what? They did! To hear that I was no longer left out because of my gender, or class, or religion lifted my spirit and my chin. I wanted to share the best I had, so I had myself and my household (yes, I had that much authority) baptized at once.

After my baptism, Paul and Silas were jailed. Later freed by a violent earthquake that loosened their chains, they came straight to my house. Of course, I welcomed them with a radiant party. The Christians gathered to hear the remarkable story, and after prison, the disciples appreciated a fine meal, luxurious tablecloths, and good wine.

My home continued to be a gathering place for Christians. It's easy to picture the word going out on the grapevine: "New letter from Paul!" They would listen eagerly as I read aloud: "Finally, beloved, whatever is true, whatever is honorable, whatever is just, whatever is pure, whatever is pleasing, whatever is commendable, if there is any excellence and if there is anything worthy of praise, think about these things" (Phil 4:8).

Prisca Speaks

(Acts 18:2, 18, 26; Romans 16:3; 1 Corinthians 16:19; 2 Timothy 4:19)

My husband, Aquila, and I were tentmakers. I never dreamt how cutting, sewing, and patching leather would lead to my great work: piecing together the fledgling Christian community like a big tent. Years later, John's prologue would describe the incarnation as God's "pitching a tent in us." Our recorded story began when Paul asked us for a job when he was new in town. He stayed with us for eighteen months in Corinth, where we had already established our business. To set the record straight, Paul didn't convert us; we were already Christian.

It caused some buzz when my name was mentioned before Aquila's (in four of six references), but let me explain. I didn't muscle in to threaten his status; it was simply a natural recognition of my leadership. He was always supportive and strong, but a man of few words. When Apollo came to Ephesus, he spoke boldly and eloquently in the synagogue. But both Aquila and I felt uncomfortable because under all that enthusiasm was a gap in his knowledge. We talked late into the night about how to handle it, and eventually decided to "take him aside." Of course, it was I who explained more accurately the story we loved, but Aquila's calm presence gave me courage and maybe assured Apollo that he wasn't being criticized by a *woman*—how embarrassing! (Acts 18:26).

I was the talker, better known, but we thought of ourselves as equals, a team. Notice how Paul refers to *our* house, not just Aquila's, as he would if he were to follow more closely the custom of our day. Oh, the male was head of the household in society, but no patriarchy for us! Everyone knew I was the feisty leader.

I wasn't spared the fear of persecution either (Rom 16:3). We risked our necks to save Paul in Ephesus, and after that, authorities seemed to know me, to sneer threateningly whenever I'd walk through town. I was so frightened, I persuaded Aquila to return to Rome. Somehow, martyrdom didn't seem the right path for us. Our work was—forgive the pun—cut out for us.

Paul did the original visioning and dramatic speeches. Then he'd turn the new converts over to us. Wise choice. Who knows better than tentmakers how to shelter newborn, vulnerable people? I'd keep them warm and dry. A tent is a flexible place, open to wind and change. Unlike more rigid structures of stone or wood, its flaps can always accommodate one more.

Rhoda Speaks

(ACTS 12:12–17)

People have been laughing at me for years. Of course, they see in me a mistake they might well have made themselves, under the circumstances.

It's crucial to understand I was a maid. That's the interesting thing about the Christian story. The people in it aren't necessarily aristocratic or highly educated or wealthy. Some are definitely bottom-of-the-heap, like me.

My parents sold me into work when I was five, and that began a long tunnel of abuse. Maybe a few blows to the head had addled my brain, I don't know. I was just grateful to work for Mary. She never beat me, and these friends of Jesus were usually gentle and forgiving. Oh, they had their crazies and their geniuses, just like any other collection of humans, but I felt more at ease with them than with any group I'd ever met. That's why I didn't want to disappoint them. I was glad they gave me a simple job like opening the door. I felt sure I could do *that*! Or could I?

I'd heard Peter speak only a few times, but he must have been an important leader, the way they carried on and prayed like mad when he got arrested. When I heard banging at the gate, I hated to leave that fervent company. I knew Peter was bound and chained in his cell, so I couldn't believe my eyes, to see him in dark shadows at the gate, and hear his voice. Indeed, I was so overjoyed, I ran to tell the others, forgetting to let him in! Some told me I was nuts, but I held my ground—I'd recognize that voice anywhere. Meanwhile, Peter patiently continued to knock, a dull thumping that accompanied the incredulous comments and dismissive conversation. Finally, in all the commotion, a few people came back with me and let him in.

They were quick to forgive, these Christians. But what meant the most was when Peter himself drew me aside a few days later and said:

> "You know, Rhoda, I haven't always been the most prayerful, reflective guy. I was more the kind who plunged in first, thought about it later. Even Jesus couldn't change who I am.
>
> "Even though I was tired that night, as I waited for you to return, wondering *if* you'd return, it gave me a chance to think. I remembered another serving girl who recognized my speech. It seemed a long time ago, that other confrontation, but the raw pain still felt fresh. How miserably I'd failed when the girl in the courtyard outside Caiaphas's palace said, 'Your speech betrays you. You are a Galilean.' You may not know this, but I denied Jesus—not only once, but three times! If I could be forgiven *that* betrayal, nothing else mattered much. I'd trust whatever door swung open next. That reminds me, didn't Jesus once say he was the gate? And what about, 'seek and you will find; knock and the door will be opened to you'? It seemed like you were gone a long time, but the memories kept me company as I wrapped my cloak close in the night chill."

I was just a maid, but this important man was telling me how *he'd* failed! And *his* betrayal made my blunder look small. Maybe I was silly, easily distracted, and unfocused, but all of us were flawed somehow, and that was OK. Once I would've been beaten mercilessly if a boss knew I hadn't opened the door to an honored guest. Now, I was hearing that the big leader had made plenty of mistakes himself!

Lightning Source UK Ltd.
Milton Keynes UK
UKHW021239240621
386084UK00005B/143

9 781626 983847